THE BOOK OF SAINTS
The Middle Era

AL TRUESDALE, Editor

BEACON HILL PRESS
OF KANSAS CITY

Copyright 2014 by Al Truesdale

ISBN 978-0-8341-3219-1

Printed in the
United States of America

Cover Design: Arthur Cherry
Interior Design: Sharon Page
Illustrations: Sharon Page

Scripture marked NIV are from the *Holy Bible, New International Version*® (NIV®). Copyright © 1973, 1978, 1984, 2011 by Biblica, Inc.™ Used by permission. All rights reserved worldwide.

Scripture marked NRSV are from the *New Revised Standard Version* (NRSV) of the Bible, copyright 1989 by the Division of Christian Education of the National Council of the Churches of Christ in the USA. All rights reserved.

Scripture references in boldface in the For Reflection sections distinguish Scripture verses quoted in the selections and prayers.

Text marked BCP is adapted from the 1979 Book of Common Prayer (New York: Church Hymnal Corporation, 1979).

Text marked Hymnary is adapted from *Hymnary.org*.

Note: To improve readability, it has been necessary to paraphrase many of the public-domain translations featured in this book. Also, prayers following the readings that do not cite an author or source are either compilations of various prayers or adaptations from the public domain.

Library of Congress Cataloging and Publication Control Number: 2013047975

"The church is nurtured by the memory of the great saints of the Christian past. But to be inspired by their deeds and enlightened by their words we need to know something about them. Truesdale brings to life the major figures of the early and medieval periods in brief biographies. *The Book of Saints: The Middle Era*, however, is not a work of history. It is designed for meditation and reflection and includes prayers and biblical readings that stir the heart as they instruct the mind."

—Robert Louis Wilken
William R. Kenan Jr. Professor of the History of Christianity Emeritus
University of Virginia

"At once devotional, educational, and transformational, Truesdale's *The Book of Saints: The Middle Era* collects and organizes treasures from the church fathers [and mothers] from AD 325 to the eve of the Reformation. After describing a theologian-pastor and his [or her] context, Professor Truesdale presents selections from the person's measured and mature walk with Christ. Each selection is followed by relevant Scripture references for further reflection and by prayers drawn from Christian tradition. The book provides rich resources for meditation . . . [and] reflection on Christ's life, the cross, his lordship, the kingdom of heaven, and the work of the Holy Spirit. The resources are timeless in their calls to move closer to our Savior and to bear fruit of the Vine."

—Karen Strand Winslow
Professor of Biblical Studies
Azusa Pacific Graduate School of Theology

"So much of Christianity has a common history, one that may be found in the lives of those who have been faithful. It is important for us to learn from them, to feel their passion, and to allow their voices to speak into our lives. Dr. Al Truesdale has brought to life a 'great cloud of witnesses,' from whom we have much to learn when it comes to our daily walk with the Lord. You will want to dig into these pages and absorb what we can learn from the past. Thank you, Dr. Truesdale, for bringing these saints to life for us today."

—Carla Sunberg
President
Nazarene Theological Seminary

O the divine mystery of the cross on which weakness hangs and divine power is revealed. Its wood has become as it were the ship of our salvation, our passage, not into punishment, but into eternal life.
—Ambrose, Bishop of Milan,
On the Holy Spirit, bk. 1, chap. 9, secs. 108-10

CONTENTS

INTRODUCTION	9
Eusebius of Caesarea	11
Athanasius	14
Hilary of Poitiers	26
Macarius-Symeon (Pseudo-Macarius)	29
The Cappadocian Fathers	43
Basil the Great	47
Gregory of Nyssa	60
Gregory of Nazianzus	66
Ambrose of Milan	70
John Chrysostom	78
Augustine, Bishop of Hippo	87
John Cassian	97
Vincent of Lérins	112
Leo the Great	121
Gregory the Great	134
Anselm, Archbishop of Canterbury	147
Bernard of Clairvaux	155
Hildegard of Bingen	165
Francis of Assisi	169
Meister Eckhart	175
John of Ruysbroeck	182
Julian of Norwich	187
Catherine of Siena (Caterina di Benincasa)	197
Thomas à Kempis	202
Theologia Germanica	212
SOURCES	**217**

INTRODUCTION

In their most universal creed, Christians affirm they "believe in one holy catholic and apostolic church" (Nicene Creed [AD 325], BCP). That is a confession of faith grounded in the church's crucified, risen, exalted, and coming Lord.

In this volume, beginning with the Council of Nicaea and continuing to the eve of the Reformation, we will learn about the holy life from persons who loved the church dearly and gave their best to ensure its faithfulness to Christ. They lived and worked during a most critically formative and often troubled period in church history. Early on, important questions were being raised and debated. Much of what we often take for granted as Christian doctrine was still unsettled. For example, how should Christian doctrine be stated to safeguard the full deity and proper identity of the Father, Son, and Holy Spirit, all without jeopardizing belief in one God? And just who is Jesus Christ? What is his relationship to the Father? Did he have a created beginning? How could he have been fully human as well as fully divine? Why is the question important anyway? And which documents should the church accept as its "Scripture"?

"We believe in one holy catholic and apostolic church." The unvarnished history of the church offers an ambiguous witness. For example, remembering the martyrs requires that we also remember a church that sometimes resorted to persecution once it gained imperial approval and power. The record that yields a unifying creed also traces a church that now seems hopelessly splintered. Often in the Middle Ages the church seemed far more committed to possessing the kingdoms of this world than to entering the kingdom of the lowly Galilean. The story of the sixteenth-century Protestant Reformation tells of doctrinal recovery. But it also reveals Protestants quickly dividing over some of the very doctrines that gave the Reformation its birth. And in the name of the Prince of Peace, less than two decades after Martin Luther posted his Ninety-Five Theses (1517), Roman Catholics and Protestants were killing many Anabaptist pacifists.

"We believe in one holy catholic and apostolic church" when many despair of the church and turn in isolation to their own private religious worlds. Nevertheless, in spite of the church's ambiguous record and its current head winds, the declaration of Jesus of Nazareth stands unchanged and unshaken: "I will build my church, and the gates of Hades will not prevail against it" (Matt. 16:18, NRSV). On the authority of the Father and by the power of the Holy Spirit, the Lord of the church will have for himself a people, his body, the fellowship of the Holy Spirit, as the vanguard of the inaugurated kingdom of God. He who despairs of the church despairs of Christ. The workings of the Holy Spirit to build the church, to make of it an evangel of the gospel of God, remain evident and undiminished. As unattractive as the church sometimes appears, it is still the bride of Christ now being prepared for the marriage supper of the Lamb.

One major difference between the fathers who appeared in volume one and the teachers who populate the pages of this volume is that after about AD 323 the church no longer faced the danger of extensive imperial persecution. Although imperial power sometimes turned against persons an emperor viewed as heretical, Christian leaders could now devote their energies to consolidating the church's faith. The Holy Spirit raised up leaders to shepherd the church. They left a storehouse of Christian treasures that can greatly enrich our faith and witness. We reverently enter their fellowship and become students as they teach us how to build on that sure foundation, which is Jesus Christ (1 Cor. 3:11).

EUSEBIUS OF CAESAREA

Eusebius, bishop of Caesarea in Palestine (ca. AD 263–339), is best known as the father of church history. He was the first to write an extended history of the church's first three hundred years. He became so much a devoted student of Pamphilius (d. AD 309) that he took the name Eusebius Pamphili (son of Pamphilius). This Eusebius should not be confused with Eusebius of Nicomedia (d. AD 341), a declared Arian.

We know little of Eusebius's early life. He was probably born in Caesarea and baptized there. His father may have been socially prominent. The reason for supposing these details is that during the persecution begun by Emperor Diocletian (r. AD 284–305), Pamphilius and others in Caesarea were martyred. Eusebius was imprisoned but not martyred, perhaps because of family influence.

He succeeded Pamphilius as head of the library at Caesarea and was probably ordained a presbyter as the persecution began to wane. Sometime around AD 313, about the time of the Edict of Milan that established imperial toleration of Christians, Eusebius became the bishop of Caesarea. He was one of the most influential bishops and theologians in the early church. Records indicate that when the Council of Nicaea (AD 325) convened, Eusebius was seated at Emperor Constantine's right hand. He delivered the inaugural address on Constantine's behalf. He so much admired Constantine that he wrote *The Life of Constantine* and *An Oration in Praise of Constantine*.

Being head of the library of Caesarea made it possible for Eusebius to write his *Ecclesiastical History*, begun during the Diocletian persecution. In it, Eusebius worked to show that with Constantine's conversion and his recognition of the church, human history had reached its pinnacle. Eusebius wrote numerous books. In his *Preparation for the*

Gospel he showed the superiority of Christianity over pagan religions and philosophies. The *Demonstration of the Gospel* showed how Jesus fulfilled Old Testament prophecy. His two-volume *Chronicle of Universal History* ranged from the call of Abraham to Constantine (AD 325).

1

No language is sufficient to express the eternity, the worth, the being, and the nature of Christ. That is why the divine Spirit asks in the prophecies, "Who shall declare his generation?" No one knows the Father except the Son; neither can anyone know the Son fully except the Father alone. For who beside the Father could clearly understand the Light that was before the world existed, the Wisdom that existed before the ages, the Living Word that was in the beginning with the Father and that was God, the true and only begotten Son of God who was before all visible and invisible creatures, the Commander in Chief of the angelic host, the Executor of the Father's will, the Creator (with the Father) of all things, the Lord and God and King of all realms of all created things, the One who has received dominion and power, with might and honor, from the Father?

EUSEBIUS OF CAESAREA, *ECCLESIASTICAL HISTORY*, BK. 1, CHAP. 2, SECS. 2-3

O MASTER, CHRIST OUR GOD, King of the ages and Maker of all things, I thank you for all the good things you have bestowed on me. You who are good and who loves all humankind, keep me under your protection and in the shadow of your wings. Grant to me with a pure conscience, even to my last breath, to partake of your holy mysteries for remission of sins and life everlasting. For you are the Bread of Life, the Fountain of holiness, the Giver of good things, and to you we ascribe glory: to the Father and to the Son and to the Holy Spirit, now and forever, and unto ages of ages. Amen.

FROM A PRAYER BY BASIL THE GREAT

FOR REFLECTION: Isa. 53:8; Matt. 11:27; Luke 1:46-55; John 1:1-18; 5:31-47; 8:12-30; 17:1-26; Eph. 1:3-14; Col. 1:15-23; 1 John 1:1-4; Rev. 19:1-8

ATHANASIUS

Except for the apostle Paul, no one has suffered more to maintain the Christian faith inviolable than Athanasius (ca. AD 296–373), bishop of Alexandria. No one realized more clearly how easily the faith can be squandered. No one was more admired by his supporters or more despised by his enemies.

One admirer, Gregory of Nazianzus (ca. AD 330-ca. 390), said that at the Council of Nicaea the Holy Spirit used Athanasius to "stay the disease of Arianism" (*Orations*, no. 21, sec. 14). But Emperor Constantius (AD 317-61), an Arian, judged Athanasius a "pestilent fellow" who was justifiably "driven from place to place, guilty of the basest crimes" (letter of Constantius against Athanasius, quoted in Athanasius, *Apology to the Emperor*, sec. 30). Because of Athanasius's unyielding defense of the apostolic faith, he was exiled from Alexandria five times. Of the forty-five years of his episcopacy, seventeen were spent in exile.

Athanasius, small of stature, with a radiant and intelligent face, was born in or near Alexandria. His writings indicate he had a sound secular education.

Around the year AD 313 he became the secretary of Alexander, bishop of Alexandria, and probably a student in the city's catechetical school. His devoted spirit, disciplined mind, acquaintance with desert ascetics, and experience of having lived through imperial persecution prepared him for stalwart and brilliant service to his Lord.

In AD 325, he accompanied Bishop Alexander to Nicaea for the great council. Though not a member of the council, somehow Athanasius's theological acumen carried the day. To him we principally owe a successful statement of the full deity of Christ now fixed in the Nicene Creed. Against the Arians who said the Son is the Father's first and highest creation, Athanasius successfully argued that Christ is of the same substance, or divine essence, as the Father.

Although the Nicene Creed affirmed our Lord's full deity, the battle to fix its confession in the church's faith continued for almost fifty years. Until his death, Athanasius labored to make orthodoxy permanent. *Against the Gentiles* and *On the Incarnation of the Word* are two of his most important writings.

2

Everywhere in nature there is order, harmony, proportion, and arrangement instead of disproportion and disarray. Therefore we should be led to recognize the Master who put together all things and produced harmony in them. Though he cannot be seen with the naked eye, yet from the order and harmony of created things it is possible to perceive their Ruler, Arranger, and King. If we were to see a city consisting of citizens different from each other in many ways, but living orderly and in unity, we would conclude that a single ruler produces concord.

The world's order and arrangement show the Word of God is its Ruler and Governor. He is one, not many. If there were more than one Ruler of creation, universal order would be lost.

If we were to hear a lyre, containing numerous strings and being played in the distance, and were to marvel at its harmony, we would conclude that it is not playing itself. Even so, the order of the universe has a single Ruler and King. By his own light the God we worship is the one Lord of creation. Most holy and above all created things, he is the Father of the Redeemer by whom the world was created. Like a ship's captain, our Lord and Savior steers, preserves, and orders all things.

ATHANASIUS, *AGAINST THE GENTILES*, PT. 3, SECS. 38, 40

O GOD, who wonderfully created, and yet more wonderfully restored, the dignity of human nature: Grant that we may share the divine life of him who humbled himself to share our humanity, your Son Jesus Christ our Lord. Amen.

"THE LITURGY OF THE WORD," THE GREAT VIGIL OF EASTER, IN BCP

FOR REFLECTION: Job 9:1-13; 12:7-12; 26:7-14; Pss. 33:1-9; 65:5-13; John 1:1-4; 2 Cor. 4:6; Heb. 1:1-3

3

The Son of God is the Father's Word and Wisdom. He acted to create all things and became incarnate to impart knowledge of his Father. Christ is the Father's very Brightness and Life. He is the Door, Shepherd, Way, Governor, and Savior over all. Having such a Son, the Father did not hide him from his creatures. Every day by means of the Son's work, the Father reveals himself. The Savior says, "I am in the Father, and the Father in me." This means the Word lives eternally with the Father who begat him. Humans in their folly rejected knowledge of and service to the Word. They honored "lords" that do not exist, instead of the eternal Lord. By making gods of things that *are not*, they have served the creature instead of the Creator. It is as if one were to praise a musical instrument but despise the craftsman who formed and tuned it. We would conclude that such a judgment would be the fruit of madness. By contrast, immortality and the kingdom of heaven are the fruit of faith and devotion to God. But first the soul must be ordered according to God's will.

ATHANASIUS, *AGAINST THE GENTILES*, PT. 3, SEC. 47

BLESSED LORD JESUS, embodying eternal grace, you are both the Messenger and message of the gospel. You lived out the gospel on earth in infinite compassion, receiving insult, injury, and death that we might be redeemed, ransomed, freed. Blessed are you, O Father, for conceiving this Way of redemption. Praise everlasting to you, Holy Spirit, for applying the gospel to our hearts. Glorious Trinity, impress the gospel upon our lives until redemption and holiness diffuse to every part. Amen.

FROM ARTHUR BENNETT, ED., *THE VALLEY OF VISION*, 35

FOR REFLECTION: John 3:31-35; 8:12-29, 42-59; 10:1-21; **14:5-14**; Rom. 1:18-32; 1 Cor. 8:4-6; Phil. 2:5-11; 1 Tim. 6:11-16

4

When speaking of the coming of the Savior among us, we must also speak of the origin of humankind. We were the reason for the Savior's descent. God created humans in his own image and willed that we should abide in *incorruption*. Not only did God create humans out of nothing, but by the grace of his Word he also freely gave us life in communion with him. Only by remaining in communion with God, by heeding his will, could humankind have preserved God's likeness and be assured of immortality. But humankind despised and rejected communion with God. People devised evil for themselves and consequently received the condemnation of death with which they had been threatened. Just as humans had been created out of nothing, because of their sin they faced an eventual return to "nothing," for bereft of the knowledge of God they would have returned to what they were when they "were not," namely, to death and disintegration. Those very transgressions called forth the Word's loving-kindness. Incarnate, he made haste to help us. For our salvation he dealt lovingly with us.

ATHANASIUS, *On the Incarnation of the Word*, SECS. 4-6

O GOD OF ALL GRACE, you have sent Christ the Savior. Now cultivate in us the faith needed to live in him, to make him our consuming desire, our hope, and our glory. May we enter Christ as a ship enters a safe harbor; may we walk in his way alone and follow him as our Guide. May we be conformed to him as our Example, receive his word as our Prophet, appeal to his intercessions as our High Priest, and serve him as our King. In the name of the Father, the Son, and the Holy Spirit, one God, forever blessed. Amen.

FOR REFLECTION: Gen. 1:26-28; 2:7-18; 6:1-8; Pss. 82:6; 95:1-7; Eccles. 7:29; Wisd. of Sol. 6:18 (Apocrypha); John 3:14-21; Rom. 1:21-22; 3:1-20; 5:14; 1 John 3:1-3

5

Death having gained power over humankind because of sin, and corruption now resting on all humans, the race was perishing. God's highest handiwork was dissolving; what it means to be "person" was disappearing. Death had a legal hold on us all, and it was impossible to evade the consequences of violating God's law. The prospects were monstrous and unacceptable. On the one hand, if after his transgression man would not die, God's word would be broken. On the other hand, it was unseemly that having once partaken of the Word of God, God's creation would descend into dissipation. It would have offended God's goodness to let what he had created waste away because of Satan's deceit.

What was God in his goodness to do? Should he allow corruption to prevail, permit death to hold us fast? If so, what would have been the benefit of God creating us in the first place? Better had we not been created than once created to be abandoned to ruin. Besides, this would have revealed weakness, not goodness and power, in God. If God had never created, no one could have accused him of weakness. To leave us hopelessly enslaved to corruption was out of the question, unacceptable, and unworthy of God's goodness.

ATHANASIUS, *On the Incarnation of the Word*, SECS. 6-7

Lord God Almighty, as Jesus' disciple I do not seek to be numbered among the rich and powerful but among those tutored by the Holy Spirit. May my supreme and abiding passion be to secure the blessings that are spiritual in nature, eternal in endurance, and pleasing in their possession. May I be completely reconciled to your will. May I not follow you hesitantly but in an abiding and holy disposition, to the praise of the triune God, Father, Son, and Holy Spirit. Amen.

FOR REFLECTION: Gen. 2:15; Matt. 18:10-14; Luke 15:1-32; Rom. 5:12-21; 2 Cor. 5:11-21; Gal. 3:19-20; 1 Pet. 1:3-12

6

For this purpose, then, the incorporeal and incorruptible and immaterial Word of God came to our realm. But he had never been far from us. He fills all things everywhere, even while remaining present with the Father. The Word condescended to shower his loving-kindness on us. He saw that we were perishing, that death reigned over us, and that corruption held us fast. God's law regarding transgression and death could not be ignored. Seeing the immense disruption that had erupted—that what the Word had authored was now dissolving in death—and seeing how we were under death's penalty, the Word of God pitied our race and had mercy on our infirmity. Our Lord refused to let death possess his creation.

The Word of God did not merely appear to be incarnate. Instead, he took for himself a body just like ours, from a spotless virgin. Being himself mighty, and the Craftsman of everything, the Word of God prepared the virgin's body as a temple for himself. In full humanity our Lord was revealed and dwelt. Taking a body like ours, and submitting to the penalty of death's corruption, Christ gave himself over to death on our behalf. He offered himself in obedience to the Father.

ATHANASIUS, *ON THE INCARNATION OF THE WORD*, SEC. 8

> *GOD WITH US, EMMANUEL,*
> *Deigns forever now to dwell;*
> *He on Adam's fallen race*
> *Sheds the fullness of His grace.*
> *Sing, oh, sing, this blessed morn,*
> *Jesus Christ today is born. Amen.*
>
> CHRISTOPHER WORDSWORTH (1807-55), HYMNARY

FOR REFLECTION: Mic. 5:2; Matt. 26:23-46; Luke 1:26-35, 38-56; 2:1-20; John 1:14; Acts 17:27; Gal. 3:15-18; Phil. 2:5-11; Col. 1:15-20

7

When godlessness and idolatry dominated the world, and knowledge of God was hidden, whose responsibility was it to teach the world about the Father? "Man," some might say. But no mere human possessed the required credibility. With all humankind smitten and confused by the devil's deceit, how could a fallen human redeem others? Or maybe the creation itself could have provided redemption. If so, then sin would not have entered in the first place. Creation was an impotent witness when humans were powerless in their sin.

The Word of God himself was required. He alone knows the whole person and gives life to the creation. He alone could fully restore knowledge of the Father. But how? One might say, by the same means the Word used in the beginning. But this was no longer certain, for humans had already failed to lift their eyes to the Father. Instead, in vanity they fixed their gaze on the creation.

So, determined to redeem humankind, the Word of God chose to dwell among us. He became incarnate and taught us through the very things he had created. We had failed to know God through his providence. But because of our Lord, we can know the Father through him.

ATHANASIUS, *ON THE INCARNATION OF THE WORD*, SEC. 14

O GOD, WHOSE WONDERFUL DEEDS of old shine forth even to our own day, you once delivered by the power of your mighty arm your chosen people from slavery under Pharaoh, to be a sign for us of the salvation of all nations. Grant that all the peoples of the earth may be numbered among the offspring of Abraham, and rejoice in the inheritance of Israel, through Jesus Christ our Lord. Amen.

"THE LITURGY OF THE WORD," THE GREAT VIGIL OF EASTER, IN BCP

✦ ✦ ✦

FOR REFLECTION: Luke 2:25-32; John 5:16-30; Eph. 1:3-12, 17-22; 2:1-10; Col. 1:9-23; 1 Pet. 1:13-24; Rev. 5:12-13; 12:10-12; 19:1-8

8

From every conceivable direction the incarnate Word showed the Father to humankind. If humans looked in awe upon the creation, they saw how creation itself confessed Christ as Lord. If their minds were swayed toward treating human beings as gods, then the Savior's works among them showed Christ to be the Son of God. No works have been performed by human beings that compare with the works of the Word of God. If people prejudiced toward evil spirits saw Christ cast out demons, they learned that the Word of God alone, not any demon, was God. And if humans who had sunk to worshipping dead heroes and the gods spoken of by the Greek and Roman poets observed the risen Christ, they admitted that those they had formerly worshipped were not gods at all.

The Lord alone is the true Word of the Father, Lord even over death. Consequently, the Son of God could be born of a virgin, live among us as fully human, be unjustly crucified, and rise again. His grace attends the works and ways of all people, so that no matter the directions their interests may lead them, Christ can meet them, recall the wayward, and lead them to the Father. Truly, Christ "came to save and to find that which was lost."

ATHANASIUS, *On the Incarnation of the Word*, SEC. 15

O LORD, we beseech you, and believe in love and much hope, that you may give to us the heavenly grace of the Spirit and that the Spirit himself may govern and guide us into the Father's perfect will. May we be refreshed in all the Spirit's many refreshments. To the glory of the Father, Son, and Holy Spirit, one God forever blessed. Amen.

MACARIUS-SYMEON, *Fifty Spiritual Homilies*, HOMILY 18, SEC. 11

FOR REFLECTION: Matt. 4:23-25; 8:14-17; Mark 3:22-29; **Luke** 4:40-41; **19:1-10**; John 10:1-21; Acts 8:7; 16:16-18

9

On the cross the incarnate Word was victorious over sin and death. So weakened has Satan become that those who were once deceived by him now mock him, for death is no longer feared by Christ's disciples. Before the Savior came, death struck terror even in the saints. But now, because of our Savior's resurrection, Christians know that death cannot finally threaten them. They know that one day the risen Lord will cause their mortality to take on immortality and make their corruption yield to incorruption.

Yes, the devil once maliciously rejoiced because of death. Now that its terror has been nullified, death is dead. Before persons become Christians, death is a terror. They play the coward in Satan's presence. But when they become disciples, their contempt for death enables them to die as martyrs, as witnesses [Greek, *martyres*] to their Redeemer.

When a mighty king defeats a tyrant, all who pass by will ridicule the vanquished. They revile him because they no longer fear his brutality. On the cross the Savior exposed and conquered the tyrant death, binding it hand and foot. Now, all who are in Christ can scoff, "O death, where is your victory? O grave, where is your sting?"

ATHANASIUS, *On the Incarnation of the Word*, sec. 27

Mighty Victim from the sky!
Hell's fierce powers beneath you lie.
You have conquered in the fight;
You have brought us life and light. Amen.

LATIN HYMN (FOURTH CENTURY AD),
TRANS. ROBERT CAMPBELL (1849), HYMNARY

✚✚✚

FOR REFLECTION: Job 17:11-16; Pss. 4:4; 55:4; 89:47; John 11:1-44; Acts 2:24; Rom. 6:1-14; **1 Cor. 15:1-58**; Rev. 1:9-18

10

If by the power of the cross, and by faith in Christ, death has been trampled down, it must be evident before the tribunal of truth that none other than Christ himself is the reason. He alone displays the trophies of triumph over death. He alone forced death to forfeit its power. When in the morning the sun rises, is there any doubt that the sun drove away the darkness? Even so, after the Savior's manifestation in the flesh, and his death on the cross, Christians know why they should hold death in contempt. For them it is quite clear that their Savior reduced death to impotence.

Day by day the Savior displays his victory in his disciples. When one sees humans, weak by nature, not fearing death's corruption, who would be so foolish as not to see that Christ gives them the victory? He who watches a serpent being walked on, knowing its former venomous power, no longer doubts its death. Or who could see children making sport of a lion and doubt its death or immobilization? Even so, now that Christ's disciples make sport of death, let no one doubt that Christ defeated death and destroyed its corruption.

ATHANASIUS, *On the Incarnation of the Word*, SEC. 29

This Joyful Eastertide,
  Away with sin and sadness!
Our Lord, the crucified,
  Has filled our hearts with gladness. Amen.
    GEORGE R. WOODWARD (1848–1934), HYMNARY

FOR REFLECTION: Rom. 8:28-39; 1 Cor. 15:1-11; Col. 3:1-17; 1 Pet. 1:3-11; 4:1-11

11

Humanity had sinned and fallen. All things were in confusion. Death prevailed and creation bore the consequences. Hell was opened; heaven was closed. Humanity was corrupted and brutalized. The devil rejoiced.

But God in his loving-kindness was unwilling that humankind, created in God's image, should perish. The Father asked, "Whom shall I send?" Heaven fell silent. But the Son of God said, "Here am I; send me." The Father willed that his Son would become incarnate, fully human, and thereby restore humanity. As one might be delivered to a physician, humankind was delivered to the incarnate Word to heal the serpent's wound. The Savior would raise what was dead and illumine humankind's darkness. Because he is the Word of God [Greek, *logos*], he would restore man's rational nature [Greek, *logikon*].

The Father had delivered all things to his incarnate Son. All things were set right, and redemption was perfected. Earth received a blessing to replace its curse; heaven was opened to the robber; death cowered; the dead were raised; and the gates of heaven were lifted up to receive the Lord.

The victorious Savior now invites all who "labor and are heavy laden." Having become poor, he makes us rich; having hungered, he nourishes us; having descended into hades, he raises us up to heaven; and dying, he has abolished death that once hung over us.

ATHANASIUS, *ON LUKE 10:22*, SEC. 2

GREAT AND MARVELOUS are your deeds, Lord God Almighty.
Alleluia, alleluia, alleluia! Amen.

FOR REFLECTION: Pss. 24:7; 49:12; **Isa. 6:8**; 63:1; **Matt. 11:28**; John 1:3; 3:35; Acts 22:1-21; Rom. 5:12-21; 8:1-17; 2 Cor. 5:11-21; Gal. 5:1-26; Eph. 1:10

HILARY OF POITIERS

In Hilary (ca. AD 300-ca. 368), bishop of Poitiers, we meet another champion of orthodox faith who, like Athanasius, suffered persecution under a Roman emperor loyal to a heretical form of Christianity. Hilary was the son of a prominent, and probably pagan, family in Poitiers (west-central France). He would eventually become the major Latin theologian during the peak of the Arian controversy. Because of Hilary's defense of orthodox doctrine, he is sometimes called the Athanasius of the West.

Hilary was educated as a pagan in philosophy and rhetoric. But he also undertook a study of the Holy Scriptures. In them he found the truth for which he had been searching. He renounced his idolatrous life and was baptized as a Christian. Because of Hilary's zeal for the faith and his education and capacity for leadership, three years after his conversion he was chosen bishop of Poitiers (AD 350). In AD 355 a council summoned by Emperor Constantius II (a son of Constantine) met in Milan. Constantius had banished Athanasius from Alexandria shortly after AD 350 because of Athanasius's unyielding defense of the Council of Nicaea. Constantius wanted his council to endorse his condemnation of Athanasius. Council members easily acquiesced. In the process they refused to hear Hilary's defense of Athanasius.

Constantius commanded Hilary to sign a condemnation of Athanasius, but Hilary refused. In AD 357, Constantius responded by banishing Hilary to Phrygia (Asia Minor). During his three-year exile, Hilary wrote numerous essays and his major work, *On the Trinity*, a powerful defense of the deity of Christ and the Trinity.

In AD 360 Constantius returned Hilary to Gaul at the request of some extreme Arians who told the emperor that Hilary was generating too much opposition against the Arians. In AD 361 Hilary returned to a joyous reception in Gaul and resumed his office as bishop. In AD 364 he traveled to Milan to debate the Arian bishop Auxentius. One account says Hilary succeeded in convincing Auxentius; another says that to protect Auxentius, the emperor drove Hilary from the city. Until his death in AD 367 or 368, Hilary worked valiantly to achieve an orthodox church and state. He is one of the doctors of the church.

12

(On the Sin of Willfulness)

True Christian doctrine is always exposed to threats from those who are either deluded by error, who misunderstand the faith, or who are governed by prejudice. Too often, our beliefs rest on pretenses rather than evidence. Where erroneous interpretations and positions have been formed, people often obstinately cling to them, for the passion of controversy is not easily eliminated. Our alleged search for truth is often obstructed because we end up trying to prove what we already believe. Such self-deception takes precedence over truth. The logic of truth is made to yield to the illogic of prejudice. This kind of "logic" doesn't motivate the will to seek the truth.

From these obstinate battles between our prejudices and what is true spring controversies in Christ's church. The truth struggles to be heard but cannot because our petulant prejudices insist on speaking and on justifying themselves. If the illogic of prejudice were not permitted to obstruct balanced thought, then true doctrine would prevail. If a desire for the truth could motivate us, instead of a desire to fortify our prejudices, then apparent contradictions in Christian doctrine would disappear. Christians would begin to desire only what is true in our faith.

HILARY OF POITIERS, *ON THE TRINITY*, BK. 10, SEC. 1

GRACIOUS FATHER, we pray for your holy catholic church. Where it is corrupt, purge it; where it is in error, direct it; where in anything it is amiss, reform it. Where it is right, strengthen it; where it is in want, provide for it; where it is divided, reunite it; for the sake of Jesus Christ, our Savior. Amen.

"FOR THE CHURCH," PRAYERS AND THANKSGIVINGS, IN BCP

FOR REFLECTION: John 17:6-26; Rom. 14:1–15:22; 1 Cor. 2:10-25; 3:1-23; 6:1-11; 13:1-13; Jude vv. 5-23

MACARIUS-SYMEON (PSEUDO-MACARIUS)

In the *Fifty Spiritual Homilies of St. Macarius the Egyptian* we are given access to rich instruction in Christian discipleship marked by mistaken identity. For centuries the *Homilies* were believed to have been written by Macarius the Egyptian (ca. AD 300-ca. 390), a recognized giant of ascetic religious practice. He was also known as Macarius the Elder, Macarius the Great, and the Lamp of the Desert. He was born in Upper Egypt. At about age thirty, Macarius retired to the Egyptian desert of Scete where he became known for remarkable powers of prophecy and healing. This Macarius should not be confused with Macarius the Alexandrian, another eminent desert father.

A few generations after the death of Macarius, the *Homilies* were ascribed to him. Although question remains as to precisely who the author was, today's patristic scholars are confident the *Homilies* came from a Syrian writer. The name of Symeon of Mesopotamia (fifth century AD) is the most favored candidate for authorship. Consequently, the author is now usually written as Macarius-Symeon or Pseudo-Macarius.

The *Homilies* made a major impact on Eastern monasticism. They have also had considerable influence on Western spirituality. Dante, John Wesley, the Jesuits, and German Pietism all testify to the *Homilies'* influence. John Wesley published an English version of twenty-two of the *Homilies* in his *Christian Library*, which was meant for use by Methodists. Wesley said of "Macarius" that he was a holy vessel of mercy who had been seasoned "with the heavenly odor of divine grace" ("Of Macarius," in vol. 1, *Christian Library*).

The original and continuing appeal of the *Homilies* resides in their challenge to all Christians to seek and directly experience the transforming and sanctifying activity of the triune God. They insist that the perfecting work of God in the life of Jesus' disciples is the essence of Christian faith. The reality of Christian discipleship is nothing less than eating and drinking the truth as it is in Jesus Christ. Although the *Homilies* do not advocate individualistic mysticism separate from the body of Christ, they uncompromisingly insist that all true Christians must "journey along the way of righteousness with an undivided will and purpose" (homily 9, sec. 13).

13

Those who want to become Jesus' disciples must cultivate the powers of discrimination. Having acquired a delicate sense of the difference between good and evil, between what is pure and what is polluted, they will live transparently before the Lord.

The power of discernment is the eye of the soul. By seeing clearly and acting accordingly, Jesus' disciples can avoid yielding to temptation. Imagine a wary traveler going through a forest where there are thorns, swampy places, and dangerous embankments. He will gather his garment close to his body for fear the thorns might rip it. But a careless person will let his garment flow wildly, paying no attention to what his eyes tell him.

Similarly, we have been clothed with the beautiful garments of the Holy Spirit. We must carefully employ the faculty of discernment as we pass through the thickets and precipices of this world. With vigilance and resolution, with discernment and discrimination, let us move the garment of the Holy Spirit this way and that to avoid Satan's entanglements.

Abide in the Lord and be guarded by his grace. Only as with our whole spirit we love the Lord, and only as we receive from heaven a love for the Holy Spirit, will we inherit the kingdom of God. The riches of the Spirit have been placed before us.

MACARIUS-SYMEON, *Fifty Spiritual Homilies*, HOMILY 4, SECS. 1-6

Dear God, I seek to know you, to love you, to rejoice in you. If I cannot do this perfectly, may I at least advance to higher degrees each day until I come more nearly to approach Christian perfection. God of truth, may my knowledge of you increase; may my love of you grow every day; may my joy in you become full. Amen.

ATTRIBUTED TO AUGUSTINE, BISHOP OF HIPPO, IN *Prayers for Today*

FOR REFLECTION: Neh. 6:10-13; 1 Cor. 8:1-3, 9; 12:1-12; 14:29; Eph. 4:14; 5:1-2; 1 Thess. 5:19-22; Heb. 12:1-13; 1 John 4:1a

14

Like a bee secretly framing her comb in the hive, grace secretly forms God's love in his people. God's grace transforms his children from bitterness to sweetness. And just as a silversmith engraves a plate, so that once complete it flashes with light, so the Lord—the divine craftsman—engraves our lives, transforms them, until the beauty of Christ shines forth.

Through many seasons and trials God's grace patiently, wisely, and mysteriously works in the lives of Christians. Then one day it becomes clear God has been perfecting his image in them all along, that they were becoming well-pleasing to the Holy Spirit. Indeed, we may patiently follow the Lord for a long time without being aware of all he is accomplishing. Think of how long it took for God to accomplish his purposes in Abraham, Joseph, and Moses, and by what pains and distresses they were proved. Let us therefore prepare to journey with the Lord along the way of righteousness with an upright mind and undivided purpose. Let us obtain through grace the promise of the Holy Spirit.

MACARIUS-SYMEON, FIFTY SPIRITUAL HOMILIES, HOMILY 9, SECS. 1-13;
HOMILY 16, SEC. 7

LET US KNOW YOU, O Lord, who knows me. Let me know you as I am known. Power of my soul, enter into it and fit it for yourself that you might have and hold it without spot or wrinkle. This is my hope, therefore do I speak; and in this hope do I rejoice. You love the truth; those who do the truth come to the light. This will I do in my heart before you and before many witnesses. Amen.

AUGUSTINE, CONFESSIONS, BK. 10, CHAP. 1, SEC. 1
(AFTER THE DEATH OF HIS MOTHER)

FOR REFLECTION: Rom. 3:21-31; 5:1-21; 2 Cor. 1:8-10; 7:1; Gal. 5:16-26; Phil. 3:12–4:1; 1 Pet. 1:3-25

15

Those who truly love the Lord, and who with strong hope and faith want to put on Christ, will not tolerate being deprived even temporarily of their passionate desire for the Lord. Being nailed to the cross of Christ, they will daily observe in themselves an advancing love for God. Being smitten with the heavenly longing and hunger for holiness and a virtuous life, their desire for the Holy Spirit is insatiable. No matter how advanced they may be in the heavenly graces and knowledge of divine mysteries, they place no trust in themselves. The more they partake of the joy of heavenly grace, the stronger their heavenly longing, and the more diligently they seek it. The more they advance in godliness, the more hungry and thirsty they are to participate and advance in divine grace. The richer they become, the more they judge themselves poor. The greater their desire for the heavenly Bridegroom, the more fit they are for eternal life and the fellowship of the Holy Spirit.

MACARIUS-SYMEON, *FIFTY SPIRITUAL HOMILIES*, HOMILY 10, SECS. 1-2

BREATHE IN ME, O Holy Spirit, that my thoughts may all be holy.
Act in me, O Holy Spirit, that my work, too, may be holy.
Draw my heart, O Holy Spirit, that I may love only what is holy.
Strengthen me, O Holy Spirit, so that I may defend all that is holy.
Guard me, then, O Holy Spirit, that I may always be holy. Amen.

ATTRIBUTED TO AUGUSTINE, BISHOP OF HIPPO, "PRAYER TO THE HOLY SPIRIT," FEAST OF ALL SAINTS

FOR REFLECTION: Ps. 31:14-24; Mark 10:32-45; Rom. 6:1-14; 1 Cor. 8:1-3; Gal. 2:17-21; 6:12-16; 1 Pet. 1:3-11; 2 Pet. 2:28–3:24

16

Many Christians are spiritually feeble. They are not advancing by patience and long-suffering toward sanctification. They have been called to live in the Holy Spirit in rest and assurance. But they have not longed for the Holy Spirit to deliver them from carnal passions. Having once received God's grace, they have allowed themselves to be deceived; they have become satisfied with a scanty advance in grace. The result is pride instead of humility.

By contrast, the person that truly loves God thinks of himself as having accomplished nothing by himself. Having been cleansed by the Spirit, sanctified in body and soul, one who loves God becomes a clean vessel for entertaining the King, even Jesus Christ. He will make us fit for eternal life, a clean dwelling for the Holy Spirit.

But a full advance in God's grace does not come all at once or without trial. Willingly and bravely enduring temptations, labors, and struggles, Jesus' disciples advance in grace and spiritual gifts and heavenly riches. Thus they become inheritors of the heavenly kingdom in Christ Jesus.

MACARIUS-SYMEON, *Fifty Spiritual Homilies*, HOMILY 10, SECS. 2-5

We petition you, our all-merciful Father . . . to bestow on us . . .
- *the spirit of wisdom to desire you above all;*
- *the gift of understanding to enlighten;*
- *the gift of discernment to follow you;*
- *the gift of strength to withstand Satan;*
- *the gift of knowledge to know good from evil;*
- *the gift of piety to clothe ourselves with love and mercy;*
- *the gift of fear [to] avoid all evil and live in awe of your majesty. Amen.*

BONAVENTURE, "PRAYERS OF ST. BONAVENTURE," LITURGIES.NET

FOR REFLECTION: Matt. 13:1-9; Luke 6:46-49; Rom. 8:18-27; 12:1-2; Eph. 3:14—4:6; 4:13—5:21; Phil. 3:1—4:1; 2 Thess. 4:1-12; 2 Pet. 3:15-18

17

Imagine there were a king who entrusted his treasure to some poor man. The man who was granted such stewardship would never claim the treasure as his own. He would always acknowledge his poverty and would be careful not to squander what belongs to another. Continually he would bear in mind that it was a mighty and gracious king who entrusted the treasure to him. He would say, "Whenever he pleases, the king can take this treasure from me."

In the same manner ought we who have received God's grace to think of ourselves. We are but stewards of his treasure. We should be humble and constantly remind ourselves of our poverty.

Now if that poor man whom the king had appointed steward were to begin to think of the treasure as his own, and if he were to become proud of the king's wealth as though it were his, the king would come and remove the treasure. Then the man would be as perilous as ever. If those who have received God's grace become puffed up in their hearts, the Lord will take his grace from them and they will be left as destitute as before.

MACARIUS-SYMEON, *Fifty Spiritual Homilies*, HOMILY 15, SEC. 27

LORD, TEACH ME TO SEEK YOU, *and reveal yourself to me when I seek you.*
For I cannot seek you unless you first teach me, nor find you, unless you first reveal yourself to me.
Let me seek you in longing, and long for you in seeking.
Let me find you in love, and love you in finding. Amen.
AMBROSE, BISHOP OF MILAN, "PRAYERS BY ST. AMBROSE," 2 HEARTS NETWORK

FOR REFLECTION: Pss. 106:1-5; 138:1-8; 139:7-18; 143:10-11; Luke 12:42-44; 1 Cor. 4:1-7; 2 Cor. 7:1; Eph. 5:19-21; Rev. 7:15-17

18

Suppose a king were to find a poor man afflicted with leprosy. And suppose instead of rejecting him, the king were to treat his wounds and heal his sores. And suppose the king were then to take the man to his castle, clothe him in purple, and make him coregent. Now this is what God will do for all who are lost in sin. He will wash their wounds and heal them. Then he will seat them at his table to dine with him. The benefits of God's grace are incomparable.

But what if the Christian who has been healed and placed at the Lord's Table were to forget his former disease? What if he were to permit sin to steal over him? He would become like a city without walls. Thieves would attack him from every direction. They would vandalize and burn his city. That is what happens when Christians who have been redeemed become spiritually careless. Satan comes in and lays waste to their spirit. He robs them of Christ's riches and scatters them in the world.

Sin is an insidious power. Unless a Christian combats it, sin will sweep him along on its tide.

MACARIUS-SYMEON, *Fifty Spiritual Homilies*, HOMILY 15, SEC. 47

Bless the Lord, O my soul, and forget not all his benefits. He has graciously forgiven all my iniquities and healed my diseased spirit. He has satisfied my hunger with good things. Let me never forget your precepts, O Lord, for by them you have favored me with eternal life. Through the Holy Spirit, may I confide in my Lord's power and love, commit my all to him without reserve, bear his image, observe his direction, enlist in his service, and be through time and eternity a testament to the efficacy of his grace. Amen.

FOR REFLECTION: Matt. 22:1-14; 25:1-46; Luke 14:25-34; 1 Cor. 1:18-31; Gal. 1:6-10; 5:1-26; Jude vv. 3-16

19

If a person is immensely wealthy, he can purchase anything he wants. He might desire rare art or jewels or to buy land. Similarly, those who seek the Lord will have access to the unlimited treasures of the Holy Spirit. The riches won by Christ will flood their lives. Out of our Lord's wealth, the Holy Spirit lavishly administers Jesus' gifts, the riches of righteousness and virtue.

By drawing on Christ's wealth, Christians amass heavenly riches. They pile up resources for living righteously in Christ Jesus and for obeying his commandments. The invisible wealth of grace has been abundantly poured into our hearts. The apostle Paul spoke of "treasures in earthen vessels." These treasures are the sanctifying power of the Holy Spirit. Christ has been made to us wisdom from God, righteousness, sanctification, and redemption.

Let us then beseech God to bestow on us the treasure of his Holy Spirit so we may be empowered to fulfill all righteousness. Poor and naked are we without the Lord's treasures. But the Holy Spirit waits to bestow Christ's wealth.

MACARIUS-SYMEON, *FIFTY SPIRITUAL HOMILIES*, HOMILY 18, SECS. 1-3

O LORD, enable us now to devote ourselves entirely to you. May we hasten to obtain the good things provided by your grace. Sanctified in soul and body, and nailed to the cross of Christ, make us fit for the eternal kingdom, glorifying the Father and the Son and the Holy Spirit, forever. Amen.

MACARIUS-SYMEON, *FIFTY SPIRITUAL HOMILIES*, HOMILY 18, SEC. 11

FOR REFLECTION: John 1:10-18; Acts 2:1-41; Rom. 12:6-8; 1 Cor. 1:30; 12:4-11, 28; **2 Cor. 4:7-12**; Gal. 5:22-26

20

The gifts of the Spirit are meant to spur Christians to perfect love toward God and man. But many Christians, like children, become fixated on spiritual gifts such as healing, revelations, and prophecies. The truth is that only in love made perfect, not in spiritual gifts, do we find the bond of Christian perfection. When a person is made complete in love, he becomes a fast-bound captive of God's grace. Short of that, he is still an easy prey to fear, failure, and anything else Satan tries.

Many Christians have received spiritual gifts and thought, "This is enough; I need no more." Consequently, many have strayed from the path of grace. They fail to see there is no *terminus* to growing in God's grace and knowing him more thoroughly. One who is perfected in love never says, "I have comprehended." He seeks to move further into God's love, further into comprehension.

In the world there is no end to learning; the scholar has tasted learning and desires more. Even so, those who have had a true taste of God freely recognize their limitations and press on into the endless life of love and grace.

Macarius-Symeon, *Fifty Spiritual Homilies*, homily 26, sec. 16-17

O Lord, by the power of the Holy Spirit, I commend my heart to your watchful care, for I know the treachery of the one who walks about as a roaring lion, seeking whom he may devour. Give me an alert discernment of his deadly schemes. Cause me to be sealed by your Spirit. Make my heart a well-tuned instrument that sounds forth your praise. Teach me the happy art of carefully attending to things temporal with a mind finely tuned to things eternal. Amen.

FOR REFLECTION: Matt. 5:48; 1 Cor. 13:1-13; 2 Cor. 7:1; **Phil. 3:12–4:1**; Col. 3:12-17; Heb. 6:1-3

21

Suppose a king were to find a poor maiden, clothed in rags. Suppose the king were to take away her soiled and ragged clothing, wash away her filth, and make her his partner? What if he were to give her a portion at his table? This is just what the Lord did when he found us wandering and stricken. He gave us the medicine of salvation, took away our garments disgraced by sin, and then clothed us with royal, heavenly garments—the garments of the triune God—all shining and glorious. He put a crown on our heads, marking us as his children. He treated us to the royal table of joy and gladness. This is the meaning and mystery of the gospel.

Therefore, let us recognize our nobility in Christ. He has exalted us to kingly dignity. We are a chosen generation, a royal priesthood, and a holy nation. The visible glory of an earthly king is perishable. But the kingdom and wealth of the gospel of Jesus Christ will never dim or pass away.

It is the faithful nature of grace to remind us that were it not for the coming of the Savior, we would still be the poor, ragged maiden deserted by the side of the road.

MACARIUS-SYMEON, *Fifty Spiritual Homilies*, HOMILY 27, SECS. 3-4

> *Praise to the Lord*, the Almighty, the King of creation!
> O my soul, praise him, for he is your health and salvation!
> Come, all who hear; brothers and sisters, draw near,
> join me in glad adoration! Amen.
>
> JOACHIM NEANDER (1680), TRANS. CATHERINE WINKWORTH (1863),
> HYMNARY

FOR REFLECTION: Rom. 7:23; 2 Cor. 3:4-6; 2 Tim. 4:6-8; 1 Pet. 2:4-10; Rev. 1:4-8; 5:10; 20:6

22

Alas for the land when there is no farmer to till it! Alas for the ship when it has no helmsman! Swept along by the surging sea, the ship will be destroyed. Alas for the soul when it doesn't have Christ as its true helmsman! Finding itself in the ocean of sin's darkness, tossed about by surges of passion and beaten by evil winds, it sinks in perdition. Alas for the soul when it doesn't have Christ to till its soil, to make sure it produces the good fruit of the Holy Spirit! Left uncultivated, it becomes overgrown by thorns and thistles.

One who plans to till the soil must have the proper implements and clothing. Just so, Christ the King, the heavenly Husbandman, in coming to humanity wasted by sin, put on true human form and carried the cross as his implement. He tilled the desolate soil of the human spirit, removed the thorns and thistles and evil spirits. He plucked up the tares of sin and burned the weeds. Then the incarnate Husbandman tilled the barren soul with the wood of the cross. He planted the fair paradise of the Holy Spirit and nurtured it to bear every fruit sweet and desirable to God.

MACARIUS-SYMEON, *FIFTY SPIRITUAL HOMILIES*, HOMILY 28, SECS. 2-3

O LORD JESUS, by the Spirit of him who raised Jesus from the dead, empower your people to embody your freedom and embrace your truth and to become messengers of the liberation from sin's tyranny you offer all persons who will seek you as the Shepherd of their souls. All glory be to the Father and the Son and the Holy Spirit, one God eternal. Amen.

FOR REFLECTION: John 1:29-34; 1 Cor. 1:17-18; Gal. 6:14; Phil. 2:8-11; Col. 1:20; 2:13-15; Heb. 12:1-3

THE CAPPADOCIAN FATHERS

(The three Cappadocian Fathers worked in harmony and are introduced as a group. Selections will follow the order of the introductions.)

Sometimes the ancient church believed correctly before it could articulate its faith in precise terms. Often, persons who misrepresented the church's faith developed conceptual language the church judged heretical. These errors often spurred the church's theologians to correct the errors and develop language that properly stated the church's faith. We are forever indebted to them.

One of the most difficult conceptual tasks was to affirm unambiguously the certainty that God is one (Deut. 6:4-5) while also faithfully expressing the deity of the Father, Son, and Holy Spirit. Christians hymned and worshipped the Father, Son, and Holy Spirit and knew that in them they had encountered the very God. How to state all this without erring in one direction or another was a formidable challenge. The task was made more urgent by a large number of persons known as Arians, who taught there is only one God, the Father. The Son is God's first and highest creation but is not God. Neither is the Holy Spirit God. The Council of Nicaea had condemned the Arian position and declared the Son and the Holy Spirit to be God, even as the Father is God. But how could this declaration be stated in convincing language?

Thankfully, a solution was provided in large part by three bishops and theologians who lived in the Roman province of Cappadocia. They are known as the Great Cappadocian Fathers. The three are Basil the Great, bishop of Caesarea (ca. AD 330-379), his brother Gregory, bishop of Nyssa (ca. AD 335-ca. 394), and their mutual friend

Gregory of Nazianzus (ca. AD 330-ca. 390). Together they made possible the victory of Nicene faith.

BASIL THE GREAT

Basil was the oldest and most distinguished of the Cappadocian Fathers. Born to a moderately wealthy and fervently Christian family, Basil was nurtured in Christian piety. His oldest sister led the life of an ascetic. Basil received a solid education, first in Caesarea and then in Constantinople and Athens. He was characterized by courage and stability. In Caesarea Basil became friends with Gregory, who would later become bishop of Nazianzus.

Basil's work as a theologian occurred in response to doctrinal errors, not as an attempt to address the entirety of Christian doctrine. In *Against Eunomius* Basil argued against the Arian teaching that because the Son is "begotten of the Father," there was a time when he did not exist. Basil responded that the Son is eternally *begotten* or generated of the Father and is eternally of the essence of God. Basil, as did Gregory of Nyssa, also wrote compellingly in defense of the full deity of the Holy Spirit.

He went on to provide a solution to the Trinitarian problem that would eventually become definitive. Basil explained that God is one *substance* or *essence* in three persons. The distinction is between the *general*, what is eternally true of each triune person, namely, deity, and what is *particularly* characteristic of each triune person. Deity is equally true of Father, Son, and Spirit. There is no division or diminishment of deity. But there is real *particularity,* a differentiation of *properties.* Fatherhood is particular, the Son is particular, and the Holy Spirit is particular, but Godhead is equally common to all three. There is a mutual indwelling of the three persons without confusion.

GREGORY OF NYSSA

Gregory, Basil's brother, is known for his theological contributions rather than for his success as an ecclesiastical administrator. He made more use of Greek philosophy than did the other two Cappadocians, even though he was aware of its danger for theology. Gregory was also more dependent on the Alexandrian theologian Origen (ca. AD 185-ca. 254). His Trinitarian thought is developed in *On the Holy Trinity* and *On "Not Three Gods."* Gregory warned that if Christians worship the Son and the Holy Spirit without affirming their full deity along with the Father, they commit idolatry. And if they do not worship the Son and the Holy Spirit as God, they are impious and clearly in conflict with the Scriptures. Gregory emphasized that far from there being division in the Trinity, there is a mutual indwelling of the three persons. He explained that Father, Son, and Holy Spirit are to be known only in a perfect Trinity, in closest union, before all creation, before all the ages, before anything we can conceive. The three persons are distinct in person, order or sequence, and activity but indistinguishable and inseparable in deity (*On the Holy Spirit: Against the Followers of Macedonius*).

GREGORY OF NAZIANZUS

Gregory, also known as Gregory the Theologian, is equally esteemed in Eastern and Western Christianity. He is numbered among the doctors of the church in the West and is one of the three Holy Hierarchs (early bishops who exceptionally shaped Christian doctrine) in Eastern Orthodoxy (Basil the Great and John Chrysostom are the other two). Gregory's theological creativity is best demonstrated in his letters, poems, and sermons. He became archbishop of Constantinople in AD 379.

Gregory's great contribution to Trinitarian theology was to show that the names Father, Son, and Holy Spirit are terms of relation, not of different essences. The relation is one of communion of essence and equal transcendence. There is but one God, the Father *of* whom are all things; and one Lord Jesus Christ *by* whom are all things; and one Holy Spirit *in* whom are all things. In addition to the different offices of the triune persons, another important distinction applies: the Father is *not begotten*, the Son is *eternally begotten* (not made) of the Father without subordination, and the Holy Spirit *proceeds*.

In sum, to the inestimable enrichment of the Christian faith, the Cappadocian Fathers taught there is one triune God in three persons—God the Father, God the Son, and God the Holy Spirit. The Godhead is their common name. All that characterizes the Trinity reveals one God. When Christians say "God," they mean Father, Son, and Holy Spirit, distinct in office but equal in glory and worship. None of the three persons is more or less God than the others, nor does one exist before the others. Though distinct and particular, the three persons are undivided in deity, will, and power. No "God" or impersonal divine substance exists above or prior to the Godhead common to Father, Son, and Holy Spirit. Christians believe in the triunity of God—an indivisible unity of three persons who have their being from, to, and in each other in an indivisible and mutual indwelling that Augustine said is properly understood as an eternal fellowship of holy, self-giving love.

Basil the Great

23

You who are Master, Lord God, and Father Almighty, it is truly meet and right and appropriate for the magnificence of your holiness that we praise you, hymn you, bless you, worship you, give thanks to you, and glorify you, the only truly existing God, and offer to you with a broken heart and the spirit of humility this our reasonable worship. You have bestowed knowledge of your truth. Who is sufficient to speak of your mighty deeds, to make all your deserved praises heard, or to declare all your wonders at any time? O Master of all, Lord of heaven and earth, and of all creation, both visible and invisible, sitting on the throne of glory, you are without beginning, invisible, incomprehensible, unbounded, and immutable. You are the Father of our Lord Jesus Christ, who is our great God and Savior, our hope, the full expression of the Father's goodness, the Living Word, true God, Wisdom before the ages, Life, Sanctification, Power, and the true Light. It is through him that the Holy Spirit has appeared, the Spirit of truth, Agent of our adoption, Pledge of our inheritance to come, the Firstfruit of eternal good things, the life-creating Power, and the Fountain of sanctification. Let every rational and intelligent creature now worship the triune God and send up everlasting doxology.

THE DIVINE LITURGY OF BASIL THE GREAT,
IN *THE DIVINE LITURGIES OF OUR FATHERS AMONG THE SAINTS*

SHINE WITHIN OUR HEARTS, loving Master, the pure light of your divine knowledge, and open the eyes of our minds [to] the message of your gospel. Amen.

JOHN CHRYSOSTOM, IN *THE DIVINE LITURGY OF ST. JOHN CHRYSOSTOMOS*,
THE ORTHODOX CHRISTIAN PAGE

FOR REFLECTION: Deut. 6:4-9; Matt. 3:16-17; 28:16-20; John 1:1; 3:16; 14:8-31; 16:12-15; 2 Cor. 13:13; Col. 2:9

24

O Master, Lover of humankind, holy are you. There is no measuring the magnificence of your holiness. In righteousness and true judgment you have provided all good things for us. In the fullness of time you spoke to us through your Son by whom you created. Being the brightness of the Father's glory, the express image of his person, and upholding all things by the word of his power, he deemed it not robbery to be equal with God the Father. Although the Word was God before the ages, he became incarnate of the holy Virgin, made this world his habitation, and sojourned among us. Emptying himself of all divine privileges, he took on himself the form of a servant. Being conformed to our humility, he transformed us in the image of his glory.

As through humans sin entered the world, so the Father's only begotten Son was born under the law that he might condemn sin by his own human life. Baptized of John and anointed by the Holy Spirit, Christ ransomed us from that spiritual death which held us captive. He opened the way for our salvation, removed from us the delusion of idols, and brought us to knowledge of the one true God.

The Divine Liturgy of Basil the Great,
in *The Divine Liturgies of Our Fathers among the Saints*

And now, O most gracious God, Father and Fountain of mercy and goodness, you have blessed us with the knowledge of the way that leads to life eternal. Let us neither trust in our own resources nor distrust your divine guidance. Open our eyes, O Father, and teach us your way. Give us a holy wisdom for discerning all things that are in harmony with your will. Amen.

Henry Scougal, *The Life of God in the Soul of Man*, pt. 3

FOR REFLECTION: Ps. 33:1-12; Isa. 6:1-7; Phil. 2:5-11; Rev. 4:6b-11; 5:13-14; 12:10-12; 15:1-4; 19:1-8; 22:12-17

25

The study of inspired Scripture is the chief way to learn how we are to live before God. There we receive instruction from men and women whose lives are breathing images of godliness. In whatever way we may feel deficient, we can devote ourselves to imitating a godly person in Scripture, just as we would procure from a dispensary the medicine applicable to our illness. For example, if we need to learn chastity, we can reflect upon the life of virtuous and self-controlled Joseph. If we need to learn patience, we can be taught by Job. When suddenly plunged from the heights of wealth to the depths of poverty, from being the father of fair children into childlessness, Job maintained the course of a righteous soul.

Just as artists repeatedly look at their model and try to transfer its features to canvas, so, too, must all who seek to live a holy life keep their eyes turned toward the lives of the saints. By imitation we must make their virtues our own.

BASIL THE GREAT, *Letters*, LETTER 2, SEC. 3

O MASTER, LOVER OF HUMANKIND, shine forth within our hearts the pure light of your divine knowledge. Open the eyes of our minds that we may understand the teachings of the gospel. Instill in us also the fear of your blessed commandments so that, having trampled all carnal passions, we may lead a spiritual life, both thinking and doing those things that are pleasing to you. Amen.

THE DIVINE LITURGY OF BASIL THE GREAT,
IN *THE DIVINE LITURGIES OF OUR FATHERS AMONG THE SAINTS*

FOR REFLECTION: Deut. 6:4-9; Luke 4:16-27; 24:13-27, 45-49; John 5:31-40; Acts 6:1-4; 1 Cor. 15:3-8

26

That farmers must labor if they want to be successful comes as no surprise. Neither are sailors shocked when they encounter storms. A laborer hired to work in the heat of summer knows he will perspire. Just so, those who walk the path of Christian holiness should not be surprised by afflictions. Farmers work hard, sailors battle storms, and laborers endure perspiration because of the things they expect to gain, not as ends in themselves. Hard work, storms, and perspiration signal something common to all human labor, and which provides consolation, namely, hope.

But sometimes hopes are dashed. Crops fail, and sailors lose their ships in storms. But the hopes of those who labor for holiness and truth will never be disappointed. Even deception by Satan cannot destroy Christian hope, for the kingdom of heaven that awaits Christians is firm and sure. Because the risen and ascended Christ is our Advocate, let us never be defeated by lies, frightened by political threats, grieved by mockery, or deceived by Satan's bait. Against all perils let us thoughtfully do battle while invoking Christ as our Advocate and nourishment.

BASIL THE GREAT, *Letters*, LETTER 18

O ETERNAL FATHER, through the redemption secured by your only begotten Son, and by the power of the Holy Spirit, fix our love on your divine perfections so that we will always have them before us and witness them being impressed upon our lives. May we be changed into your image, from glory to glory. Lift our eyes to our Lord's uncreated beauty and goodness, and set all our affections upon it. Inspire in us by the Holy Spirit a holy fidelity to this high and noble calling. Amen.

HENRY SCOUGAL, *The Life of God in the Soul of Man*, PT. 2

FOR REFLECTION: Luke 8:1-15; 12:22-34; John 11:17-27; 14:1-4; Phil. 1:21; 3:12-16; Col. 1:21-23; Rev. 22:7-17

27

That Christian athlete Paul, desiring that we not rest on how well we have lived in the past, says, "Forgetting those things that are behind, and reaching forth to those things that are before, I press toward the mark for the prize of the high calling." This is generally true of human life. A person is no better for having eaten yesterday if he cannot satisfy his hunger today. In the same way, the soul gains nothing by yesterday's virtue unless it is followed by a virtuous life today. It is not he who begins well, but he who ends well who comes to Christian perfection. That person is approved by God.

We are passing through snares and treading in perilous places. Let us not try to master the Christian life all at once. When you have gained mastery in one area, begin to wage war against another hurdle. Beware of overconfidence. Meet each temptation with patient endurance. Let us not be rash in speech, quarrelsome, or covetous of vainglory. Always be ready to learn and slower to teach. Finally, it is much better to speak of the lives of godly people than to always talk about the sins of others.

BASIL THE GREAT, *Letters*, LETTER 42, SECS. 1-2

O ETERNAL AND MOST GRACIOUS GOD, prompt us to consider your bountiful mercies. Teach us to fear every approach of sin and to live with jealous attention to your will. Establish in us a constant assurance of your grace. Help us to fly to you at the approach of every temptation, assured that you will lift us up and keep us from falling. Grant this, O Father, for the sake of him who knows our infirmities—your Son, our Savior, Christ Jesus. Amen.

JOHN DONNE, *Devotions*, PT. 1, PRAYER 1

FOR REFLECTION: Prov. 6:5; Ezek. 18:24; Luke 14:28, 30; **Phil. 3:13-14**; Heb. 10:19-25; 12:1-13; Jude vv. 17-23; Rev. 2:3-22

28

(Who is the Holy Spirit?)

In conformity with the Scriptures, let me tell you who the Holy Spirit is. Just as our baptism was of the Holy Spirit, even so by him we make our confession of faith. Just as our baptism was given by our Savior in the name of the Father and of the Son and of the Holy Spirit, even so, in accordance with the Creed (of Nicaea) we offer the doxology to the Holy Spirit as God. We glorify the Holy Spirit together with the Father and the Son because of our conviction that his is none other than the divine nature that defines the Father and the Son.

Even a slight knowledge of Scripture teaches us that creatures are not God and are not to be worshipped. But the Holy Spirit liberates enslaved creatures. How then could he be one of the creatures? Life must be given to creatures. But the Holy Spirit bestows life. Creatures must be taught. But the Holy Spirit teaches. Creatures need to be sanctified. But the Holy Spirit sanctifies. Creatures *receive holiness*. But the Holy Spirit *is holy* by nature. We do not permit what is holy by nature to be separated from the blessed Trinity.

BASIL THE GREAT, *LETTERS*, LETTER 159, SEC. 2

BLESSED HOLY SPIRIT, come this day and fill me with your holy gifts. Let my weakness be penetrated by your strength. Assist me in all my responsibilities. Protect me in temptations, and console me in afflictions. Enlighten me in my ignorance, and advise me in my doubts.

Graciously hear me, O Holy Spirit, and pour your light into my heart, mind, and soul. Assist me to live a holy life and to grow in goodness and grace. Amen.

FROM "PRAYERS TO THE HOLY SPIRIT," 2 HEARTS NETWORK

FOR REFLECTION: John 6:63; 14:26; Acts 2:38-39; Rom. 5:18-19; 8:1-18; 15:14-19; 1 Cor. 2:6-15; 12:4-6; 2 Cor. 13:14

29

(The following probably came from a sermon preached at the beginning of Lent.)

Beware that you do not limit fasting to abstinence from food. Real fasting involves much more. It means abandoning all evil. "Loose the bands of wickedness." Forgive your neighbor the mischief done against you. Forgive those who trespass against you. As important as it might be to refrain from eating meat, it is more important that you not devour your brother.

Do you abstain from wine and then imbibe outrages? Do you wait until evening before eating food but spend the whole day in the courts seeking your own interest? Woe to those who refuse wine but then become intoxicated with anger.

Whatever sets the soul against God's peace should be considered intoxication, the opposite of true fasting. Let us remember who we have been ordained to receive as our Guest, the One who promised that he and his Father would make their abode with us. Do not permit any form of intoxication to enter your soul, and in turn slam the door against the Lord. Do not let Satan move into your stronghold. Just as smoke drives away bees, even so intoxication of the soul drives away the Holy Spirit and his gifts.

Basil the Great, first sermon on fasting

O Lord God, you have shown us what is good and what you require of us. Cleanse us of all that is false and superficial, all that is contrary to what you have shown us of yourself; calm our passion for things of this world, and cause your holy virtues to be instilled in us. Let the depths of our souls be opened to your grace and correction so that we may be shepherded by your righteous staff. Amen.

FOR REFLECTION: 1 Sam. 7:2-6; Neh. 9:1-37; **Isa.** 51:21-23; **58:3-14**; Matt. 5:16-18; 24:42-44; Luke 4:1-13; John 14:23

30

I am astonished by the inventions of excessive luxury. The vehicles are countless. Some are for conveying goods, others for carrying their owners, and all are covered with brass and silver. Horses' pedigrees are recorded as though they were human. Some carry their haughty owners around town, some are for hunting, and some are just hacks. Scarlet cloths make the horses as merry as bridegrooms. Of servants whose task it is to satisfy human extravagance, there are agents, stewards, gardeners, craftsmen, and confectioners. Add to that cooks, butlers, huntsmen, sculptors, painters, and entertainers. There are baths in town and in the country. Houses shine with every kind of marble. Floors are mosaic, and ceilings are gilded. If any section of the wall escapes the slabs of stone, it is embellished with painted flowers.

You who dress your walls but let your neighbor go naked and hungry, how will you answer the eternal Judge? You who harness your horses with splendor and yet despise your brother if he is poorly dressed, you who let your excess wheat rot in the fields instead of feeding the hungry, you who hide your gold and then despise those who are distressed, how will you answer God on the day of judgment? How will you justify your excesses to him?

BASIL THE GREAT, "AGAINST THE RICH," HOMILY 7

O GOD OF THE OPPRESSED AND BROKEN, we are all beggars in need of your grace. We recognize that love is the first and greatest commandment and that love and compassion for the poor is the law's most excellent form. Help us to open our hearts to the poor, to those suffering from evil. Amen.

GREGORY OF NAZIANZUS, FROM "THE GREGORY OF NAZIANZUS PRAYER," AMOS HOUSE COMMUNITY

FOR REFLECTION: Amos 5:11-15, 21-27; Matt. 25:31-46; Luke 16:19-31; Acts 3:1-10; James 2:1-13; 5:1-6

31

(In Praise of the Psalms)

The book of Psalms is a treasury of sound teaching for every need. The Psalms heal the sick while preserving the healthy. They can tame passions that try to overwhelm us. The Psalms accomplish all this with a musical persuasiveness and gratification that fosters wise and wholesome thought. The Holy Spirit knew it would be difficult to attract humans to goodness, that the scale of life is weighted toward pleasure, and that we tend to neglect what is holy. Knowing this, what plan did the Spirit adopt? He combined the delight of melody with his teaching so we might drink deeply of his instruction. He acted as a wise physician administering distasteful medicine by first putting honey around the lip of the cup. This is how the melodious music of the Psalms has been designed. While we are singing, the Spirit is educating us. Being easily inattentive, we do not readily receive an oracle delivered by a prophet or apostle. But the Psalms are sung in our houses and travel with us through the streets. A person might tend to be as savage as a wild beast. But no sooner is he soothed by psalm singing than he goes home tamed and calmed by the music of the Psalms.

BASIL THE GREAT, "PRAISE OF THE PSALMS,"
PREFACE TO HOMILY ON PSALM 1

O SPIRIT OF THE LIVING GOD, empower me through the Holy Scriptures to hold fast to the rudder of the gospel of Jesus Christ. Guide me constantly lest the vehement waves of temptation drive me from the way of the Lord. Instruct me daily in the steersman skill to set my course by your holy will. Amen.

BASIL THE GREAT, "ON THE BEGINNING OF THE PROVERBS," HOMILY 12

FOR REFLECTION: 2 Tim. 3:16; types of psalms: (1) *lament psalms*: Pss. 44; 55; 130; 137; (2) *thanksgiving*: Pss. 34; 63; 107; (3) *hymnic psalms*: Pss. 33; 66:1-12; (4) *liturgical psalms*: Pss. 45; 87; 115; 132; (5) *community psalms*: Pss. 19:7-14; 133

32

When the apostle Paul "thanks God through Jesus Christ," and again says that "through him" we have gained "access into this grace wherein we stand and rejoice," he identifies the blessings bestowed on us by the Son of God. The grace of God comes from the Father, through the Son. In turn, the Son brings us to the Father. By saying that through the Son he "received grace and apostleship," Paul declares that the Father's good gifts proceed through the Son. By declaring that through the Son we have access to the Father, he shows how the Father accepts us and makes us "members of the household of God."

Does the Son's gracious abode in us distract from his glory? No. Instead, reciting the Son's benefits motivates us to glorify him. Scripture uses many terms to speak of Christ. Sometimes it uses terms that describe the Son's triune deity. He is called the true Son, the only begotten God, the Power of God, and God's Wisdom and Word.

Because the Son works to bestow the Father's riches, he is called Shepherd, Physician, Bridegroom, Way, Fountain, Bread, and Rock. To those who affirm his righteous royalty he is King; to all who walk the straight path of his commandments, Christ is the Door.

BASIL THE GREAT, *On the Holy Spirit*, CHAP. 8, SEC. 17

Our God, save your people and bless your inheritance; protect your church, Christ's body; sanctify those who love the beauty of your house; glorify them in return by your divine power; and do not forsake us who hope in you. Amen.

JOHN CHRYSOSTOM, IN *The Divine Liturgy of St. John Chrysostomos*, THE ORTHODOX CHRISTIAN PAGE

FOR REFLECTION: Ps. 107:20; Matt. 3:10; 9:12, 15; 21:5; 27:54; John 10:9, 12; 14:6; **Rom. 1:2-8**, 16; 2:4; **5:2**; 1 Cor. 1:24; 10:4; **Eph. 2:19**; 3:10; Phil. 2:9-11; Heb. 1:1-4; Rev. 21:6

33

Baptism has two goals. One is that the body of sin might be destroyed. It must never again bear the fruit of sin and death. The second is that we will live daily by the Holy Spirit and bear the true fruit of holiness. The water of baptism receives the old self as though the water were a tomb. In the second movement, the Holy Spirit pours in the life-giving power. He raises us, frees us from sin's death, and restores us to communion with God. This is what it means to be born again of water and the Spirit—death carried out in the baptismal water, and new life created through the Spirit. By immersion in the name of the Father, Son, and Holy Spirit, the great mystery of baptism occurs. There is no grace or power in the water itself; grace and power come from the Spirit's presence. Baptism is fulfilled in peace and fellowship with God. In training us for what follows baptism, the Lord makes clear the manner of life the gospel requires—the law of gentleness, enduring wrong, and freedom from covetousness and the defilement that comes from craving pleasure. Through a set purpose of obedience to the gospel we gain a foretaste of what will follow the resurrection.

BASIL THE GREAT, ON THE HOLY SPIRIT, CHAP. 15, SECS. 35-36

KEEP ME, O LORD, for I am yours by creation; guide me, for I am yours by purchase. By your care keep me from offense against you. In evil make me as innocent as a child, but in understanding, godliness, and godly fear make me an adult in Christ, readily furnished and instructed in every good work. Amen.

JEREMY TAYLOR, "AN EXERCISE TO BE USED AT ANY TIME OF THE DAY,"
IN *THE RULE AND EXERCISES OF HOLY LIVING*

FOR REFLECTION: Matt. 3:11; Rom. 6:1-10; 15:29; 1 Cor. 3:13; Gal. 3:23-29; Eph. 5:25-33; 1 Pet. 3:21

34

When we consider how our great God and Redeemer, Jesus Christ, acted to redeem humankind, we see how everything he accomplished was attended by the Holy Spirit. Whether we consider the blessing of the patriarchs, God's care for his people during the age of the law and the prophets, the victories God gave to his people, the miracles performed through the saints, or the incarnation of the Word in Jesus of Nazareth, everything has been accomplished through the power of the Holy Spirit.

The Spirit was active in the holy conception of Mary and was with the Lord from his infancy. Jesus was anointed and led by the Holy Spirit. Jesus was led into the wilderness by the Spirit to be tested. Jesus drove out demons "by the Spirit of God." After Jesus rose from the dead, he did not abandon his disciples but sent the Holy Spirit at Pentecost.

The Holy Spirit orders the church by how he administers Christ's gifts. Even the revelation of the mystery of the gospel is the peculiar work of the Holy Spirit. When the blessed and only Sovereign judges the world in righteousness, even then the Holy Spirit will have an assignment to discharge.

BASIL THE GREAT, *ON THE HOLY SPIRIT*, CHAP. 16, SECS. 39-40

O GOD OF UNCHANGEABLE POWER AND ETERNAL LIGHT: Look favorably on your whole church, that wonderful and sacred mystery; by the effectual working of your providence, carry out in tranquility the plan of salvation; let the whole world see and know that things which were cast down are being raised up, and things which had grown old are being made new, and that all things are being brought to their perfection by him through whom all things were made. Amen.

"THE LITURGY OF THE WORD," THE GREAT VIGIL OF EASTER, IN BCP

FOR REFLECTION: Isa. 61:1-3; **Matt.** 3:17; 4:1; **12:28**; Luke 4:1-2; 24:45-49; John 1:33; 14:15-31; 15:26; Acts 2:22; 10:38; 19:11; Rom. 8:1; 2 Thess. 2:13; Titus 2:13

35

(The Titles of the Holy Spirit)

We understand the Spirit's deity and incomparable power by considering his titles, the magnitude of his office, and the good gifts he bestows on us. He is called Spirit, as in "God is spirit." He is called holy, even as the Father and Son are holy. For all creatures before we can call them "holy" must be made holy by something beyond themselves. But holiness is the essential nature of the Holy Spirit. For this reason the Holy Spirit is the Sanctifier, not one who needs to be sanctified. He is called good, even as the Father and the Son are good. His goodness is his essence. The Holy Spirit is called upright, even as "the Lord is upright." He is Truth and Righteousness. As God, the Spirit is steadfast in faithfulness. The Holy Spirit is called the Paraclete, Advocate, just as Christ is Comforter. "I will ask the Father," Jesus said, "and he will give you another Comforter." The Spirit is called royal, the Spirit of truth, and the Spirit of wisdom.

You see that the Holy Spirit bears names in common with the Father and the Son. He receives these titles because of his deity and from his close communion with the Father and the Son.

BASIL THE GREAT, *ON THE HOLY SPIRIT*, CHAP. 19, SEC. 48

CREATOR SPIRIT, by whose aid
The world's foundations first were laid,
Come, visit every humble mind;
Come, pour thy joys on humankind;
From sin and sorrow set us free,
And make thy temples worthy thee. Amen.

JOHN DRYDEN (1631–1700), HYMNARY

✛✛✛

FOR REFLECTION: Pss. 43:10; **92:15**; 143:10; Isa. 11:1-3; **John 4:24**; **14:16-17**; 16:12-15; 2 Cor. 3:7-11; Phil. 4:7; 2 Thess. 2:13-15; **1 John 1:20**; 5:6

Gregory of Nyssa

36

When we employ the noun "man," we use it to indicate a nature common to and shared by all persons. Peter, for instance, is no more *man* than Andrew. "Man" is the essence or substance of humanity. Let's place Paul, Silas, and Timothy together. If we explore the human essence of each of them, it will be the same for all three. But when we speak specifically of Paul, we intend to describe his distinguishing characteristics or properties, no matter how much he has in common with Silas and Timothy.

Now, transfer these distinctions to the Trinity. Whatever is true of the divine essence of the Father is also true of the deity of the Son and of the Holy Spirit. Deity is one and the same essence and sovereignty—one God—in the Father, Son, and Holy Spirit, even though each person has his own characteristic activities. One member of the Trinity is neither more nor less God than the others. There is no break or void in the divine essence and mutual harmony of the Father, Son, and Holy Spirit.

GREGORY OF NYSSA, LETTER TO BASIL,
IN BASIL THE GREAT, *LETTERS*, LETTER 38

THOU, WHOSE ALMIGHTY WORD
Chaos and darkness heard,
And took their flight,
Hear us, we humbly pray;
And where the gospel day
Sheds not its glorious ray,
Let there be light! Amen.

JOHN MARRIOTT (1780–1825), HYMNARY

✣✣✣

FOR REFLECTION: Matt. 28:19; John 1:3-8; 6:32-59; 7:25-44; 14:5-13; 16:13-15; Rom. 8:9; 1 Cor. 2:12; 12:11; 2 Cor. 13:14; Col. 1:15-17; Heb. 1:3

37

Many who come to the grace of baptism are either self-deceived or led astray by others. They receive baptism without truly becoming new creatures in Christ. Baptism is meaningless if we continue to live as we did before. How is it possible for a person in whom there is no change in his distinguishing features after his baptism to think that he is anything more than he was before? It should be clear to anyone that the purpose of baptism is to bear witness to a new birth that renovates and changes our natures. Human nature alone cannot produce this change. What does regeneration entail?

The washing of regeneration involves doing away with the sinful things that marked our unregenerate lives. If baptism has been applied to the body, but the soul is not cleansed from sinful passions and affections, and if that person continues to live as before, then the water of baptism was nothing more than water. In no way does the gift and work of the Holy Spirit appear in such a person. If the deformity of sin continues, then I cannot see how he has been changed at all. Hear the apostle Paul: "If a man thinks himself to be something, when he is nothing, he deceives himself." What we have not become by the grace of regeneration, that we are not.

GREGORY OF NYSSA, *THE GREAT CATECHISM*, CHAP. 40

O FATHER OF ALL MERCIES, God of all comfort, you order all things in wisdom. Accomplish in us all that is well-pleasing to you. May the grace of our Lord Jesus Christ and the fellowship of the Holy Spirit come upon us. Advance us toward all that is holy for the perfecting of the church and to the praise of the glory of your name. Amen.

GREGORY OF NYSSA, *LETTERS*, LETTER 13

✠ ✠ ✠

FOR REFLECTION: Isa. 1:16; John 3:5-8; Rom. 6:1-14; **Gal. 6:3**; Eph. 4:1-6; 2 Pet. 2:1-22; Jude vv. 3-16

38

The gospel says of those who have been born again, "As many as received him, to them he gave power to become the sons of God." The child born of a parent evidences a kindred nature. If you have become God's child, then manifest in yourself the One who by grace gave you new birth. The marks that permit us to recognize God must characterize those who are born of the Father. For example, God opens his hand and fills every living thing with his good pleasure. He forgives transgressions. He is good to all and does not vent his anger on us. He is a righteous Lord, and there is no injustice in him. If your life is marked by such things as these, then you are a child of God. But if you continue to manifest the characteristic marks of sin, then it will be foolish to babble on about your birth from above. Prophecy will speak against you: "You are a 'son of man,' not a son of the Most High. You 'love vanity and seek after lies.' Do you not know in what way man is 'made admirable'?" Only by holy living are we made admirable as the children of God.

GREGORY OF NYSSA, *THE GREAT CATECHISM*, CHAP. 40

O LORD, by your grace you bestow mercy on all persons and despise nothing you have created. Remember now how frail we are and that you are our Father and God. Mercifully forgive trespasses, and take away our hearts of stone. Give us hearts that delight to do your will, to love and adore you. Kindle in our hearts the fire of the Holy Spirit. Inspire our prayers so that they may be such as please you. Amen.

AMBROSE, BISHOP OF MILAN, "A PRAYER BEFORE MASS (THURSDAY),"
CATHOLIC ONLINE

FOR REFLECTION: **Pss. 4:2-3**; 7:11; 145:16; Joel 2:13; Matt. 6:1-34; **John 1:10-13**; Rom. 8:17-19; Gal. 3:26-28; 1 Pet. 2:1-12

39

For the joyous sacrament of baptism to be effective it must be manifested in subsequent purity of conduct. Baptism in no way changes our physical characteristics. What is merely physical can't provide the needed proof. However, there must be a confirming manifestation by which the new person can be recognized. By what tokens can the old be distinguished from the new? Such tokens can emerge only if a person is committed to regeneration. The old accustomed way of life must yield to a new way of life. Only then will others know that something truly new has happened.

The old self was undisciplined by godliness. It grasped for what belonged to others, used abusive language, lied, and was slanderous. By contrast, let us now be marked by true regeneration: a life ordered by godliness, by sobriety, by contentment with our own possessions, and by ministering generously to the poor. Let the new person be truthful, courteous, and approachable. Just as light dispels darkness, even so the old self will disappear when adorned with righteousness. As God's children, let us examine our heavenly Father's characteristics. Then, by the Spirit, let us fashion ourselves in his likeness. Let us now demonstrate by transformed lives that we have been adopted by God's grace.

GREGORY OF NYSSA, *On the Baptism of Christ*

In your hearts enthrone him;
There let him subdue
All that is not holy,
All that is not true. Amen.

CAROLINE MARIA NOEL (1817-77), HYMNARY

FOR REFLECTION: Matt. 5:43-47; Luke 15:1-24; John 4:4-26; Acts 22:2-21; Rom. 3:21-26; 5:1-11; 6:3; Col. 3:12-17

40

After our adoption as the children of God we can expect that the devil will plot against us more intensely and violently than ever. He will be envious as he beholds the newborn child of God journeying toward the heavenly city. Don't be surprised when the devil hurls fiery temptations against us. He will seek to rob us of our new adornment, just as he robbed Adam and Eve. When the devil attacks, we ought to repeat the words of the apostle, "As many of us as were baptized into Christ were baptized into his death." If we have been conformed to Christ's death, then the old sinful self has become a corpse, pierced through by the javelin of baptism. Let us command the devil to flee, for what he seeks is dead. Once, the old self was his ally, but no longer. It has been crucified with Christ. It can no longer lust for wealth, slander, or revile others. The new self has learned how to pass by the things of this world and hasten on to the things of heaven. In the same way Paul testifies that the world is crucified to him, and he to the world. This must be the defining disposition of those who have been born anew.

GREGORY OF NYSSA, *On the Baptism of Christ*

Ever-Living God, Father of all mercies, may my wealth be to become rich in holy virtues so that by them I can serve you and please you in all truth. Give me holy virtues for the honor and glory of your name. Make me steadfast in a faith that works through love. May the faith my tongue confesses be manifest in holy conduct. Amen.

ANSELM, ARCHBISHOP OF CANTERBURY, *Book of Meditations and Prayers*, MEDITATION 18, SEC. 90

FOR REFLECTION: Num. 25:7-9; Ps. 119:11; **Rom. 6:3**; 12:21; 1 Cor. 10:11-13; 2 Cor. 5:11-15; Gal. 6:14; James 4:7-10; 1 Pet. 5:8-11

41

Let us now worship the Giver of our great salvation. Truly, O Lord, you are the pure and eternal Fountain of all goodness. You were just in turning against our sins. But in loving-kindness you had mercy on us. You were hated; still, you reconciled. You were cursed, yet you blessed. Because of our sin you banished us from the garden, yet you restored us to communion with you. You stripped off our fig leaves, our unseemly covering, and then clothed us in costly garments. You opened prison gates and released condemned captives. You sprinkled us with clean water and purged our pollution.

No longer need we hide when we hear your voice, convicted and cowering in the thicket. We who were heirs of sin now have reason to rejoice. Heaven may now be entered. The whole creation that was once in conflict with itself has been knit together in friendship. Now we can join the angels in signing praises to you.

Now we sing the hymn of joy inspired by the Holy Spirit. "Let my soul be joyful in the Lord, for he has clothed me with a garment of salvation."

GREGORY OF NYSSA, *On the Baptism of Christ*

O my God, may I remember all your mercies. Let my bones be bedewed with your love, and let them say to you, "Who is like you, O Lord?" You have shattered the bonds of my captivity. I will offer you the sacrifice of thanksgiving. I will declare to all how you set me free. When all who worship you hear my testimony, they will exult, "Blessed be the Lord in heaven and earth, great and wonderful is his name." Amen.

AUGUSTINE, BISHOP OF HIPPO, *Confessions*, BK. 8, CHAP. 1, SEC. 1

FOR REFLECTION: Pss. 35:10; 41:13; 45:1-21; 72:19; 89:52; 106:48; 146:1-2; 147:1-20; 150:1; **Isa. 61:10**; Eph. 1:15-23; 1 Tim. 6:11-16; Jude vv. 24-25

Gregory of Nazianzus

42

On this day Christ rose from the dead. May he today renew me by the Holy Spirit, clothe me with the new humanity, and bestow upon me his new creation.

On Good Friday the Lamb was slain and the doorposts were anointed. Egypt bewailed her firstborn, the destroyer passed over us, the seal of blood was dreadful and revered, and we were walled in by the precious blood. Today, Easter, we have escaped Egypt and from Pharaoh. Now, no one can restrain us from celebrating a feast to the Lord our God—the feast of our departure. We feast, not with the old leaven of malice and wickedness, but with the unleavened bread of sincerity and truth. We carry with us nothing of the old Egyptian leaven.

On Good Friday I was crucified with Christ; today I am glorified with him. Yesterday I died with Christ; today I rise with him. Yesterday I was buried with my Lord; today from the tomb I rise with him.

Let us offer to him *ourselves*, the possession most precious to God. In the triumphant Christ let us recognize our dignity, let us honor our Archetype, and let us know the power of the mystery and why Christ died.

Gregory of Nazianzus, "On Easter and His Reluctance [to accept ordination to the priesthood]," Oration 1, secs. 2-4

O Christ, bring again our daylight; day returns with you!
Hell today is vanquished; heaven is won today! Amen.
Venantius Honorius Clementianus Fortunatus (ca. AD 530–609),
trans. John Ellerton (1868), Hymnary

FOR REFLECTION: Exod. 12:1-30; Isa. 65:5; Matt. 28:1-10; Mark 16:1-13; Luke 24:1-12; John 1:35-36; 20:1-18; Acts 2:14-36; 1 Cor. 5:8; Rev. 5:6-14

43

We have learned to believe in the deity of the Son of God from the Son himself. He was baptized as man, but he forgives sins as God. He was tempted as man, but he conquered as God, and he bids us to be of good cheer because he overcame the world. He hungered, but he fed thousands. He is the Bread of Life, the very Bread of Heaven. He thirsted, but he proclaimed, "If any man thirsts, let him come to me and drink." He even promised that fountains would flow from those who believe. He grew weary, but he offers rest for all who are weary and heavy laden. He grew heavy with sleep, but he walked lightly upon the sea and rebuked the storm. He pays taxes but from a fish's mouth. More, he is even the King of those who required taxes of him. He is derided as being a Samaritan, but he saved the one who fell among thieves. He is accused of being of the devil, but legions of demons flee at his command. He even witnesses the prince of the demons falling like lightning. He prays but hears the prayers of others. He weeps, but he causes tears to cease. As man, he weeps over Lazarus, and then as God, he raises him from the dead.

GREGORY OF NAZIANZUS, "ON THE SON," ORATION 29, SEC. 20

> LET ALL MORTAL FLESH KEEP SILENCE,
>   And with awe and reverence stand;
> Ponder nothing earthly minded,
>   For with blessing in his hand,
> Christ our God to us approaches
>   Our full homage to demand. Amen.

ADAPTED FROM THE DIVINE LITURGY OF JAMES THE HOLY APOSTLE (CA. AD 150-200), TRANS. GERARD MOULTRIE (1864), HYMNARY

✦✦✦

FOR REFLECTION: Matt. 3:13; 8:24; 9:6; 11:28; 14:25, 30; 17:24; Luke 8:28-33; 9:30; 10:17-20, 30; **John** 6:10; **7:37**; 8:48; 11:43; 16:33; 19:19

44

We have learned to believe in the deity of the Son of God from the Son himself. He was betrayed and sold for very little, but he redeems the world at the price of his own blood. As a sheep he is led to the slaughter, but he is Shepherd of Israel, and of the whole world. As a sacrificial lamb he is silent, yet he is the eternal Word of God. He is bruised and wounded, and yet he heals every disease. He is lifted up and nailed to the cross, yet he saved even the robber crucified beside him. On the cross, he wrapped the visible world in darkness. He is given vinegar to drink, but he is altogether the Sweetness that overcomes the bitter taste of sin. He lays down his life but has power to take it again. He rends the veil of the temple and thereby opens for us the doors of heaven. He dies, but he gives life, and by his death he destroys death. He is buried, but he rises again. He goes down into hell, but he releases the captives. He ascends to the Father and will come again to judge the quick and the dead.

What he was (God), he continued to be; what he was not (man), he took to himself.

Gregory of Nazianzus, "On the Son," oration 29, secs. 19-20

> *King of Kings, yet born of Mary,*
> *As of old on earth he stood,*
> *Lord of Lords, in human vesture,*
> *In the body and the blood,*
> *He will give to all the faithful*
> *His own self for heavenly food. Amen.*

Adapted from The Divine Liturgy of James the Holy Apostle (ca. AD 150-200), trans. Gerard Moultrie (1864), Hymnary

FOR REFLECTION: Song of Sol. 5:16; Isa. 53:7, 23; Matt. 6:28; 26:15; 27:51; Luke 23:43; John 1:23; 2:1-11; 10:7-18; 11:43; 19:19; 1 Pet. 1:19

45

(On the Birthday of Our Lord)

Christ is born; glorify him. He comes from heaven; let us go out to greet him. The Lord is born of a virgin. Let the heavens rejoice, and let the earth be glad, for Christ, who was first of heaven and is now of earth. Let us rejoice with trembling because of our sins and with joy because of our salvation. Who will not worship him, the Beginning and the End?

Now our darkness is past; the light has dawned. Egypt is covered with darkness, and Israel is enlightened by a pillar of fire. Let us who sat in darkness now look to the full light of knowledge. Old things have passed away; all things have become new. The letter of the law has yielded to the Spirit of life. The shadows have fled, and the Truth has replaced them.

Clap your hands all you people, for unto us a child is born, unto us a Son is given. Let us acclaim the power of this day, for the Son of God has become the Son of Man. This is our festival, the coming of God to man, that we might go forth to God. Having cast off the old Adam, let us now put on the New. As we died in Adam, let us now live in Christ.

GREGORY OF NAZIANZUS, "ON THE THEOPHANY," ORATION 38, SECS. 1-2, 4

SING, OH, SING, THIS BLESSED MORN;

. . . .

God himself comes down from heaven;
Sing, oh, sing, this blessed morn,
Jesus Christ today is born. Amen.

CHRISTOPHER WORDSWORTH (1807-55), HYMNARY

FOR REFLECTION: Exod. 14:20; Pss. 47:1-4; 96:1; Isa. 9:6; Jer. 31:31-40; Mal. 4:1-6; Matt. 1:18-25; 3:3; Luke 2:1-20; 1 Cor. 1:23; 5:17; 15:22; 2 Cor. 5:17; Eph. 4:22-24; Col. 2:11; Heb. 13:8

AMBROSE OF MILAN

"To Milan I came, to Ambrose the bishop, known to the whole world as among the best of men, your devout servant, whose eloquent discourse did then plentifully dispense unto your people the flour of your wheat, the gladness of your oil, and the sober inebriation of your wine" (*Confessions*, bk. 5, chap. 13, sec. 23). That is part of Augustine's testimony on the role Ambrose (340-97), bishop of Milan, played in Augustine's conversion. Augustine, a teacher of rhetoric, had intended to examine Ambrose's fame as an eloquent speaker. Instead, he was captured by the bishop's proclamation of the gospel and his kindness. Ambrose, Augustine said, taught "salvation most soundly" (sec. 23).

Ambrose came from a prominent Roman family that had early embraced the faith. Some family members were among the martyrs. Before the death of Ambrosius, Ambrose's father, in AD 354, Ambrosius was chief magistrate of Gallia (France, Britain, and Spain) and Tingitana (Africa).

On the death of Ambrosius, Ambrose's mother assumed responsibility for mentoring her children in Christian piety. She made sure Ambrose received an excellent education in Greek language and literature. After completing his secular education, Ambrose studied law and became distinguished for his eloquence and legal argumentation. Before long he gained the notice of Emperor Valentinian, who appointed him consular governor of Liguria and Aemilia, with residence in Milan, a city roiled by conflict between Arians and those faithful to the Nicene Creed.

Ambrose governed efficiently and gained the respect of the citizens. On the death of a tyrannical Arian bishop named Auxentius, Valentinian instructed Ambrose to oversee election of a new bishop. Completely to the surprise of Ambrose, the people and clergy who were gathered at the forum called for the election of Ambrose as bishop, a sacred office for which he had not prepared. Although an orthodox believer, Ambrose had not been baptized. An orthodox bishop baptized him, and at age thirty-five, reluctantly, Ambrose became bishop of Milan. He served for twenty-three years. In the memory of Christianity, there is unambiguous agreement that Ambrose was the "perfect model of a Christian bishop" (*Catholic Encyclopedia*, s.v. "St. Ambrose").

46

(In Praise of Silence)

What should we learn first? How to be silent. Only then will we learn to speak. Otherwise, our words might condemn us before anyone can defend us. We should not rush into condemnation that results from speaking rashly when we can just as easily avert the danger by remaining silent. We have seen persons fall into error by speaking, but scarcely have we seen anyone fall into error by remaining silent. It is more difficult to learn how to be silent than it is to know how to speak. Most persons speak because they don't know how to be silent. In fact, often a person speaks even when speaking profits him nothing.

The Law says, "Hear, O Israel: The Lord your God." Notice that the instruction is not to "speak" but to "listen." A person is wise, then, if he knows how to remain silent. The wisdom of God has told us that the Lord gives the tongue of learning so that we might know when it is proper to speak. So we may recognize a person as wise if he has received from the Lord knowledge of when to be silent and when to speak.

Let us bind up our words that they not run riot. Sobriety of mind has reins by which the mouth should be guided.

AMBROSE, BISHOP OF MILAN, ON THE DUTIES OF THE CLERGY,
BK. 1, CHAP. 2, SECS. 5, 7; CHAP. 3, SEC. 12

> *BE THOU MY VISION*, O Lord of my heart;
> Naught be all else to me, save that thou art;
> Thou my best thought, by day or by night,
> Waking or sleeping, thy presence my light. Amen.
>
> IRISH HYMN (CA. EIGHTH CENTURY AD),
TRANS. MARY E. BYRNE (1905), HYMNARY

FOR REFLECTION: Deut. 6:4; Job 5:21; Ps. 39:1; Prov. 10:11, 19-20; Eccles. 3:1-8; Isa. 50:4; Matt. 12:36; Eph. 4:29-32; James 2:26-27; 3:1-12

47

If we pay heed to the counsel regarding silence, we will be mild, gentle, and modest. For in guarding our mouths and restraining our tongues, and by not speaking before we examine what we intend to say, by pondering and weighing our words, we will certainly be practicing modesty, gentleness, and patience. We will not blurt out in anger or displeasure, display evidence of passion, or show that the flames of lust burn in our language or that wrath is present in us. Our words should demonstrate grace and moral fortitude.

Satan lays his plans when we show him that passions control our inner selves. He will seize an opportunity to wound us with our own sword. Far better to perish by the sword of others than by our own! Satan, our enemy, tests our armament before he attacks. If he sees by our speech that we are disturbed, he will hurl his darts with the intent of raising a crop of quarrels. If we utter improper words, he sets his trap into which he places the bait of desired revenge. Taking the bait, we end up in his trap and tightly draw the death knot around us. If we realize that Satan is lurking nearby, we ought to give extra attention to what we are about to say lest we open the door for him to rush in.

AMBROSE, BISHOP OF MILAN, ON THE DUTIES OF THE CLERGY,
BK. I, CHAP. 4, SECS. 14-16

O SOVEREIGN LORD, we beseech you to repel the assaults of sin and to gladden our minds with the radiance of the Holy Spirit. May we partake of the mercies you have set before us through your only begotten Son, our Savior. Amen.

THE DIVINE LITURGY OF THE HOLY APOSTLE AND EVANGELIST MARK
(BEFORE AD 200)

FOR REFLECTION: Pss. 39:1-10; 90:3; Luke 22:55-60; Eph. 6:10-18; 1 Thess. 5:4-11; 1 Pet. 1:3-7

48

Be on your guard; stand firm in the faith; be people of courage. Courage, or fortitude, is a very important Christian virtue. It is allied with other Christian virtues. It protects their beauty. Fortitude watches over the power of discernment and fights against all vices with unrestrained valor. Courage bravely endures dangers, is stalwart in its opposition to destructive pleasures, and is hardened against distracting allurements. To such enticement, fortitude refuses to extend a greeting or lend an ear. It will not permit itself to be subverted by love for money. Rather, it flees from greed as humans flee the plague.

AMBROSE, BISHOP OF MILAN, *ON THE DUTIES OF THE CLERGY*,
BK. I, CHAP. 39, SEC. 202

O LORD AND MASTER OF MY LIFE! Take from me the spirit of sloth, faintheartedness, lust of power, and idle talk. But give rather the spirit of chastity, humility, patience, and love to your servant. Yea, O Lord and King! Grant me to see my own errors and not to judge my brother. For you are blessed unto ages of ages. Amen.

THE LENTEN PRAYER OF EPHREM THE SYRIAN, ORTHODOX WIKI

FOR REFLECTION: Prov. 28:1; Ezek. 2:1-7; Dan. 3:16-18; Acts 4:1-22; 1 Cor. 16:13-14; 2 Cor. 3:17-18; Phil. 1:27-30; 1 Tim. 6:11-16; 2 Tim. 1:1-10

49

Nothing so quickly subverts Christian fortitude than becoming enamored with this world's goods. Often when Satan and his hosts are being put to flight, a Christian warrior is defeated because he permits himself to be diverted and infatuated by the enemy's spoils. If a Christian warrior abandons the fight and begins to plunder the enemy's booty, he will end up bringing Satan back to the battle after he had fled the field, and the Christian warrior may die among those he should have vanquished.

Fortitude, then, must repulse, must crush, the foul plague of being attracted to Satan's wares. They must hold no attraction for us. True virtues remain faithful to themselves. Fortitude should wage war on vices as though they were trying to poison virtue. But in doing so, fortitude must guard against self-glory.

Did holy Job lack any of this? He correctly assessed the dangers that menaced his safety and never permitted greed or the desire for pleasures or lusts to arise in his heart. He retained his trust in God. Job would not let vice accompany virtue.

AMBROSE, BISHOP OF MILAN, *ON THE DUTIES OF THE CLERGY*,
BK. I, CHAP. 39, SECS. 203-4

BREATHE ON ME, BREATH OF GOD,
   Fill me with life anew,
That I may love what thou dost love,
   And do what thou wouldst do. Amen.

EDWIN HATCH (1835-89), HYMNARY

✦✦✦

FOR REFLECTION: 1 Kings 11:1-13; 2 Kings 5:1-27; Luke 12:35-38, 42; Eph. 6:11-17; Phil. 3:12–4:1; 2 Tim. 4:9-10; James 3:13–4:10

50

With the Eucharist, Christ feeds his church. By Christ's food the church makes continual progress in God's grace. Christians must protect the deep meaning of the Eucharist, a meaning that only the bride of Christ can know. The Lord's Supper is the secret garden, the seal and fountain of the Lord. Beholding so great a grace, let us come to Christ's feast.

One of the ways we protect the mystery of the Eucharist, the food of Christ, is through holy lives. An unholy life pollutes the food of Christ and violates the church's purity as Christ's bride. The bride of Christ can also pollute the food Christ gives us in the Eucharist by speaking carelessly about our faith to unbelievers. Guardianship of the mystery of Christ, of our faith, occurs in lives characterized by Christian integrity. Only then can our testimony endure unblemished. Only through fidelity to the mystery of Christ can the church expect to repel the storms that are sure to buffet her.

AMBROSE, BISHOP OF MILAN, *ON THE MYSTERIES*, CHAP. 9, SECS. 55-56

ALMIGHTY AND EVER-LIVING GOD, I approach the sacrament of your only begotten Son, our Lord Jesus Christ. I come sick to the Doctor of life, unclean to the Fountain of mercy, blind to the radiance of eternal Light, and poor and needy to the Lord of heaven and earth. Lord, in your great generosity, heal my sickness, wash away my defilement, enlighten my blindness, enrich my poverty, and clothe my nakedness. Amen.

FROM A PRAYER OF THOMAS AQUINAS,
IN "PRAYERS BEFORE HOLY COMMUNION," DIOCESE OF SUPERIOR

FOR REFLECTION: Ps. 34:9; Matt. 25:14-30; Luke 22:1-46; 1 Cor. 10:3, 14-22; 11:17-33

51

The highest goal of virtue is to achieve the greatest possible measure of good. Gentleness is the virtue that most completely serves this purpose. It is the loveliest of all because it does not destroy even those it condemns. It is the only virtue that truly leads to the increase of the church, which the Lord purchased with his own blood. By imitating our Lord's loving-kindness, gentleness seeks the redemption of all persons. In its presence the hearts of sinners will neither quake nor descend into despair.

He who seeks to amend human weakness must let weakness weigh on himself, just as the good shepherd carried the lost sheep on his shoulders. Restraint must temper righteousness. Why should anyone whom you despise, and who thinks that your righteousness judges him to be an object of contempt, offer himself to you for healing?

The Lord Jesus refreshes and does not cast off. He came in meekness, had compassion on us, called us to himself, and did not frighten us away. "Come to me," Jesus said, "all you that labor and are heavy laden, and I will refresh you."

Clearly those who practice a harsh and proud righteousness cannot be counted among Jesus' disciples. Advocates of such righteousness seek God's mercy while denying it to others.

AMBROSE, BISHOP OF MILAN, *CONCERNING REPENTANCE*, BK. 1, SECS. 1-3

I THANK YOU, O HOLY TRINITY, for through your great goodness and patience you have not been angry with me. When I was prostrate in despair, you raised me to glorify your name. Enlighten me to meditate on your words, understand your commandments, do your will, and hymn you in heartfelt confession. Amen.

"MORNING PRAYERS," IN PRAYER BOOK OF SAINT VLADIMIR RUSSIAN ORTHODOX CHURCH, PRAYER 1

FOR REFLECTION: Job 14:4; Ps. 51:2; Eccles. 7:17; **Matt. 11:28**; Luke 7:36-50; 11:32; 15:3-5; 18:9-14; John 8:1-11; Gal. 5:22-26; 1 Thess. 1:2-10

JOHN CHRYSOSTOM

Often when we think of persecution of God's people, we have in mind those outside the faith. But often persecution of the faithful arises from within the church. This was true of John Chrysostom (ca. AD 347–407), the doctor of preachers, who died while on his way into exile. John, called Chrysostom (Greek, *chrysostomos* [golden-mouthed]) because of his eloquence, was born to Christian parents in Antioch of Syria during a time of considerable unrest and division in the church. His father was a high-ranking army officer who died shortly after John's birth. John's mother, Anthusia, assumed responsibility for raising John and his older sister. She instructed him in piety and sent him to the best schools, where he was educated in classical culture.

When Chrysostom was about twenty-three years old, he met the earnest, mild, and winning Bishop Meletius. He was so captivated by this godly man that he forsook his study of classical culture and began to give himself to the study of Scripture. Around AD 370 he was baptized. About AD 374 Chrysostom began to lead the life of an anchorite in the nearby mountains. But in AD 386, because of poor health, he was forced to abandon his life as an ascetic and return to Antioch, where he was ordained a priest. In AD 398 Chrysostom became the bishop of Antioch. He would go on to become one of the most stalwart spokesmen for orthodox faith in the early church, a defense that cost him dearly. He is a doctor of the church.

Chrysostom was repeatedly buffeted by enemies inside the church. One enemy was Theophilus, the contentious patriarch of Alexandria, who resented the fact that Chrysostom had given refuge to some priests fleeing Theophilus's anger. Before his death, Theophilus repented of his false accusations against Chrysostom. Chrysostom's most formidable enemy was Empress Eudoxia. She could not abide the apostolic freedom and authority of John's preaching. In spite of the pope's support of Chrysostom, Eudoxia sent him into exile. But his enemies in the church were not satisfied. So they had Chrysostom banished to the most remote eastern part of the empire. On the way into exile, he died, September 14, 407.

52

How great the gain of humility! How great the damage of pride! Consider two charioteers, the Pharisee and the publican. They were driving two chariots, each pulled by two horses. The Pharisee's horses were Righteousness and Pride. The publican's horses were Sin and Humility. Although the Pharisee's chariot was assisted by fasting and tithes, and although the publican was a poor charioteer, the Pharisee fell behind. The publican was contrite and admitted himself a sinner. The Pharisee boasted that he had no vices. Why did his chariot fall behind? Because, although he was not restricted by greed and robbery, the mother of all evils—Self-Righteousness and Pride—reigned over him. His pride could not be tolerated. So he fell behind.

The Pharisee was like a ship that had traveled the ocean and survived many storms. Then at the mouth of the harbor the returning ship crashed against the rocks and lost its cargo. After having endured the labors of fasting and working hard to develop virtue, he failed to master his pride. Going home after prayer, he should have enjoyed great gain. Instead, because of self-righteousness, his ship lay wrecked in the harbor.

JOHN CHRYSOSTOM, *HOMILY CONCERNING LOWLINESS OF MIND*, SECS. 1-2

> *COME, DEAR REFRESHMENT of those who languish;*
> *Come, Star and Guide of those who sail amid tempests.*
> *You are the Haven of the tossed and shipwrecked.*
> *Come now, Glory and Crown of the living,*
> *As well as the Safeguard of the dying.*
> *Come, Sacred Spirit;*
> *Come, and make me fit to receive you. Amen.*

FROM AN INVOCATION BY AUGUSTINE, BISHOP OF HIPPO, IN *PRAYERS FOR TODAY*

FOR REFLECTION: Ps. 69:32-33; Prov. 15:33; 16:19; Matt. 5:1-12; 11:29; 18:2-4; Luke 9:46-48; 18:9-14; 1 Cor. 11:21-31

53

Material riches are vulnerable to robbers, false accusers, and dishonest servants. And even if material riches escape these perils, they often bring the greatest ruin on their owners by provoking envy in others and by breeding countless storms of trouble. But the spiritual riches of Christ escape all this mischief and are superior to them all. They laugh to scorn would-be thieves, slanderers, false accusers, and even death itself. Even death cannot deprive Christians of Christ's riches. On the contrary, at death those riches become even more secure. They go along with Christians on their journey to heaven; they are deposited in the future life.

Astonishingly, no matter how zealously Jesus' disciples make withdrawals, his treasury never becomes depleted. Spiritual wealth resembles fountains of water: they continue to be abundant even though many people draw from them. Although Christ's riches have made countless persons rich, they remain in their original state of perfection. Yet Christians continue to withdraw as much and as often as they like.

JOHN CHRYSOSTOM, *Homily on the Paralytic Let Down through the Roof*, SEC. 1

May the God of mercies and the God of all comfort, who disposes all things in wisdom for the best, visit us by his grace and comfort us by himself, working in us that which is well-pleasing to him, and may the grace of our Lord Jesus Christ rest on us, and the fellowship of the Holy Spirit, that we may have healing amid all tribulation and affliction, and advance toward all that is good, for the perfecting of the church, for the edification of our souls, and to the glory of his name. Amen.

GREGORY OF NYSSA, *Letters*, LETTER 13

✟✟✟

FOR REFLECTION: Rom. 9:22-24; 11:33-36; Eph. 1:7-10, 18; 2:1-9; 3:8, 16; 4:7-8; Phil. 4:14-19; Col. 2:9-12; Rev. 5:11-12

54

He who would approach the holy mystery of the Lord's Supper must be spiritually attentive. He must be cleansed from all foolish allegiances, full of self-restraint and preparation. He must banish all interests foreign to the character of God. He must cleanse and prepare himself as if he were preparing to entertain a king.

We must no longer lust for the things of this earthly life or be enslaved to the luxuries of the physical table or to costly raiment. For in Christ you already possess the most excellent of raiment, the best spiritual table, your true home, your source of life, your head, and your glory from on high. The mystery of God is that we have not only become Christ's sisters and brothers but also the children of God and members of Christ's body.

Knowing all these things, let us show our thankfulness by our conduct. Consider the greatness of Christ's sacrifice. Keep the gift of Christ clean from all covetousness and deceit. Guard your tongue in purity against crude and abusive language, against all blasphemy and perjury. Let us honor the mysteries of Christ with the same honor with which God honors his Son.

JOHN CHRYSOSTOM, *First and Second Instruction to the Catechumens*, FIRST INSTN., SEC. 2; SECOND INSTN., SECS. 1-2

Remember, O Lord, your mercies that are from everlasting. Stretch out your hand to draw me to yourself, for I cannot come to you except you draw me with cords of love. Make me a servant pleasing to you, for I cannot please you in any other way. Grant that my supreme love and desire will be for you. Convert me completely to your praise and glory, and perfect me in all you have begun. Amen.

ANSELM, ARCHBISHOP OF CANTERBURY, *Book of Meditations and Prayers*, MEDITATION 8, SEC. 36

FOR REFLECTION: John 6:56-57; 15:4-5, 15; 1 Cor. 4:7; 11:17-33; 2 Cor. 4:1-18; 11:2; Gal. 3:27; Eph. 1:22; 4:15; 1 Tim. 6:3-10, 15-21

55

Jesus' disciples said, "Teach us to pray." In response, he gave them this prayer: "Our Father, which art in heaven, hallowed by your name, your kingdom come, your will be done, as in heaven, so on earth. Give us this day our daily bread, and forgive us our debts as we also forgive our debtors. And lead us not into temptation." Later, Jesus showed the disciples what he meant by "lead us not into temptation." In the garden he prayed, "Father, if it be possible, let this cup pass away from me." He thereby taught his disciples not to plunge into dangers with overconfidence. By his own prayer, Jesus taught self-restraint and moderation. He instructed us to seek deliverance from distress. But if this is not permitted, we should acquiesce in what seems good to God. That is why Jesus prayed, "Nevertheless, not as I will, but as you will." Just as Jesus instructed, let us petition that we may never enter into temptation. But if we do, let us ask God to give us patience and courage, and let us honor his will over our own. Then we will pass through this present life with safety and obtain the heavenly blessings he has prepared.

May we all arrive at this by the favor and loving-kindness of our Lord Jesus Christ, with whom be to the Father, together with the Holy Ghost, glory, might, and honor, now and forever, world without end.

JOHN CHRYSOSTOM, *Homily on Matthew 26:19*, SEC. 4

Our heavenly Father! Hear our prayer;
Thy name be hallowed everywhere;
Thy kingdom come; thy perfect will,
In earth as heaven, may all fulfill. Amen.

JAMES MONTGOMERY (1771–1854), HYMNARY

FOR REFLECTION: Pss. 28:7; 37:4-6; 46:10; Prov. 3:6; **Matt.** 4:1-25; **6:9-13**; **26:36-46**; **Luke 11:1-4**; Rom. 15:13; 1 Cor. 12:8-10; Phil. 4:4-13

56

(Chrysostom addressed the following to those under his care who were careless about Christian discipleship and church attendance.)

We do not commit leadership of the church to people just because they happen to govern nations and cities or because they command armies. Leadership of the church depends on a different kind of government, one more excellent than governing the empire requires.

What kind of leaders should those who enter the church of God expect to find? They must first be trained to govern their own passions, to rule over lusts, to control anger, to temper ill will, and to subdue pride. The emperor may be seated on his throne and may wear his crown. But he is not as accomplished as one who places reason on the throne to govern passions. What profit is royal gold-trimmed clothing if a person remains captive to his passions? What is the benefit of external freedom if one's conscience has been reduced to disgraceful servitude?

The prophets and apostles stand ready to help us expel the reign of passions and place them under governance more powerful than the empire itself. But those who deprive themselves of such care will suffer greater harm than can come from any other quarter.

JOHN CHRYSOSTOM, *HOMILY TO THOSE WHO HAD NOT ATTENDED THE ASSEMBLY*, SEC. 4

ALMIGHTY GOD, you have built your church upon the foundation of the apostles and prophets, Jesus Christ himself being the Chief Cornerstone: Grant us so to be joined together in unity of spirit by their teaching, that we may be made a holy temple acceptable to you; through Jesus Christ our Lord. Amen.

"PROPER 8," COLLECTS: CONTEMPORARY, IN BCP

FOR REFLECTION: Rom. 12:1-8; 1 Tim. 3:1-13; 4:1-16; 5:17; 2 Tim. 3:1-9; 4:1-8; Titus 2:1–3:11

57

(Chrysostom discusses how to exit a church service.)

Unless we put into practice what is preached in God's house, then preaching profits us nothing. Zeal for hearing the gospel must bear fruit in our conduct. Indeed, it is good to listen to divine proclamations. But doing so is pointless unless the fruit of righteousness follows.

Even if you say nothing after leaving church, your demeanor should show others what you gained; your very conduct should be enough to exhort others. Leave God's house as though you are leaving a sacred shrine, as though you were returning from heaven, composed and reflective. Let anyone who sees you returning from God's house, including an enemy, gain some impression of the benefits. Consider the privilege of having participated in Christ's mysteries. Consider the fellowship of the Holy Spirit in which you cried, "Holy, holy, holy!" Let those whom you meet in the world learn you have participated in the chorus of the Seraphim and that you are numbered as a citizen of the heavenly commonwealth. By your conduct in the world let those you meet know that you have been in the presence of Christ.

JOHN CHRYSOSTOM, *HOMILY TO THOSE WHO HAD NOT ATTENDED THE ASSEMBLY*, SECS. 4-5

ALMIGHTY GOD, by the Passover of your Son you have brought us out of sin into righteousness and out of death into life: Grant to those who are sealed by your Holy Spirit the will and the power to proclaim you to all the world; through Jesus Christ our Lord. Amen.

"THE LITURGY OF THE WORD," THE GREAT VIGIL OF EASTER, IN BCP

FOR REFLECTION: Ps. 4:16-17; Matt. 5:1-16; 7:15-29; Mark 4:1-25; 9:42-50; John 15:22; Rom. 2:13, 19-21; James 1:18-27

58

Come, let us cleanse the robes of our souls, and with self-denial make ready to enter the Gospels. There we will find the King, seated on his throne in unspeakable glory, with angels and archangels and the triumphant saints standing before him. In the Gospels we will encounter the city of God, namely, "the church of the firstborn, the spirits of the just, the general assembly of the angels." Therein we will see displayed the trophies of the cross—all the spoils won by Christ. They are glorious and conspicuous. Death and sin have been crucified, and Christ has thereby gained riches for the church. In the Gospels we will observe how the tyrant has been bound and how the devil's league of captive demons follows the conquering Christ. We will see how the robber's hiding place has been broken up. We will marvel over what a wondrous thing it is that God incarnate came to earth in battle array, even to hell itself. The devil, attempting to overthrow the Lord, will also be there. You will watch as Christ destroys death through death, extinguishes the curse of sin through the curse of the cross, and puts an end to Satan's dominion.

Let us rouse ourselves, for the Gospel gates are opening. Let us enter with joy and trembling.

JOHN CHRYSOSTOM, HOMILY ON MATTHEW 1:1,
HOMILIES ON THE GOSPEL OF ST. MATTHEW, HOMILY 2, SEC. 1

O LORD JESUS, through the Holy Scriptures, truly enlivened by the Holy Spirit, reveal to us in full the mystery of the gospel of God—its wisdom and power, its justification and sanctification. Give us the strength we need to show to others that we are Christians and that you alone can fill the human heart with grace, peace, and joy. Amen.

FOR REFLECTION: Jer. 33:6-16; Rom. 8:28-39; Eph. 3:7-21; 6:10-18; Col. 2:13-20; 1 Tim. 3:16; **Heb.** 7:4; **12:22-23**; 1 Pet. 3:18-22; Rev. 1:9-18

AUGUSTINE, BISHOP OF HIPPO

No theologian since the apostle Paul has had a greater impact on the church in the West than Augustine, bishop of Hippo (AD 354–430). He is the greatest of the Latin fathers and the greatest theologian of grace and love since Paul. His theology was shaped, not in peaceful abstraction, but in the heat of battle as he fulfilled his episcopal responsibility as shepherd of the faith and the faithful. He lived when the empire in the West was in advanced decay and when many pagans blamed Christians for the decline.

Fortunately, not only do we know the more public features of Augustine's life, but through his *Confessions* we also gain entrance to his interior life, to the riveting process by which God led a brilliant but licentious pagan to conversion and holiness and to the fountains of his developed theology. Augustine was born in Tagaste, Numidia, North Africa. The prayers of his Christian mother, Monica, played a major role in his conversion. His father was a pagan and remained so until late in life. One childhood instance in which Augustine stole pears later played a role in his examination of the nature of evil.

At seventeen, Augustine went to Carthage to study rhetoric, where he became one of the city's most eloquent speakers. In uninhibited detail, he tells us his life as a student was accompanied by abandonment to sexual lusts. His concubine bore him a son, Adeodatus. His study of Cicero provoked a search for truth, a search that led through allegiance to Manichaeism and Neoplatonism. While still a Neoplatonist, he came under the influence of the eloquent and sainted Ambrose, bishop of Milan. Ambrose was able to resolve Augustine's objections to Christianity. In *Confessions* Augustine chronicles how God's grace closed him in and transformed him from a fleeing rebel to a consummate lover of God. *Confessions* maps the consequences of a sinful love of creation and a transforming love for God. In time, Augustine would develop a doctrine of the Trinity that explains the Father as the Lover, the Son as the Beloved, and the Holy Spirit as the Love between the Father and Son.

59

All God's commandments hark back to love. The apostle Paul says, "Now the end of the commandment is love, out of a pure heart, a good conscience, and a faith unfeigned." If one obeys a commandment because of fear of punishment or some other fleshly impulse, rather than out of love, it is not performed as it should be. Love in this instance means love for God and love for our neighbor. Indeed, "on these two commandments hang all the Law and the Prophets" and, we might add, the gospel and the apostles. The love being considered here is that which the Holy Spirit sheds abroad in our hearts. From the gospel and the apostles comes the voice, "The end of the commandment is love," and "God is love."

Therefore, whatsoever God commands is rightly obeyed only when measured by the standard of love—for God and for our neighbor. This truth applies in the present age and in the world to come. Now we love God in faith and then, at his appearing, in sight.

AUGUSTINE, BISHOP OF HIPPO,
ENCHIRIDION (HANDBOOK ON FAITH, HOPE, AND LOVE), CHAP. 121

YOU ARE GOD: we praise you;
You are the Lord: we acclaim you;
You are the eternal Father:
All creation worships you.
To you all angels, all the powers of heaven,
Cherubim and Seraphim, sing in endless praise:
Holy, holy, holy, Lord, God of power and might,
Heaven and earth are full of your glory. Amen.

"YOU ARE GOD," DAILY MORNING PRAYER: RITE II, IN BCP

✠ ✠ ✠

FOR REFLECTION: Matt. 5:48; **22:34-40**; John 15:9-23; Rom. 13:8-14; 1 Cor. 13:1-13; **1 Tim. 1:3-7**; **1 John 4:13-21**

60

(Augustine says that before his conversion he did not know the following truth. Consequently, he loved the "lower beauties" as ends in themselves and sank further into darkness.)

If physical things please you, praise God because of them; turn back upon the Creator your love for them. If not, the things that please you will displease the Father because you love them apart from him. If the beauty of the human spirit pleases you, let it be loved in God, for human life is temporary and changing. But if you love human life in God, then humanity will be firmly established.

Carry to God as many persons as you can. Say to them, "Let us love God, let us love God, for he is the Creator and he is not far from us. Our God did not create and then abandon his creation. No, the creation is made secure in him."

Say to them, "See, there is our God!" He is present wherever truth is loved. He lives within the human heart. Let transgressors return to God and cling to their Creator. Stand with him, and you will stand fast. Rest in him, and you will find rest. Your love will become bitter if it is not anchored in him. Why walk a toilsome path apart from God? Why seek life in the land of death. A blessed life is to be found where Life itself is.

AUGUSTINE, BISHOP OF HIPPO, *CONFESSIONS,* BK. 4, CHAP. 12, SEC. 18

O GOD, the glorious company of apostles praises you.
The noble fellowship of prophets praises you.
The white-robed army of martyrs praises you.
Throughout the world the holy church acclaims you. Amen.

"YOU ARE GOD," DAILY MORNING PRAYER: RITE II, IN BCP

FOR REFLECTION: Ps. 91:1-16; Luke 19:1-9; John 5:24-27; Acts 9:13-19; 2 Thess. 3:1-5; 1 John 2:1-11

61

(The conclusion of Augustine's long journey to Christ.
He and a friend entered a little garden.)

No one could hinder the hot contention within me. You, Lord, knew how it would end. I knew the evil person I was but not the good thing I was shortly to become.... I was troubled in spirit, angry that I had not already embraced your will and covenant, which my bones cried out to enter, praising it to the skies. I was speaking and weeping in bitter contrition, when, lo! I heard from a neighboring house the voice of a child, "Take up and read; take up and read." Instantly, my countenance changed. I interpreted the child's voice to be a command from God to open the volume (Romans) and read the first chapter I should find. I seized the volume, opened it, and read the first section: "Not in rioting and drunkenness, not in chambering and wantonness, not in strife and envying; but put on the Lord Jesus Christ, and make no provision for the flesh to fulfill its lusts." No further did I need to read, for instantly, by a light as it were of serenity infused into my heart, all my darkness vanished.

AUGUSTINE, BISHOP OF HIPPO, *CONFESSIONS*, BK. 8, CHAPS. 8–12

You, O CHRIST, are the king of glory,
The eternal Son of the Father.
When you became man to set us free,
You did not spurn the Virgin's womb.
You overcame the sting of death
And opened the kingdom of heaven to all believers.
You are seated at God's right hand in glory.
We believe that you will come and be our judge. Amen.

"YOU ARE GOD," DAILY MORNING PRAYER: RITE II, IN BCP

FOR REFLECTION: Matt. 19:21; John 3:1-8; Acts 9:1-19; **Rom. 13:8-14**

62

(Augustine offers his doxology after his conversion.)

"O Lord, I am your servant and the son of your handmaid [his mother, Monica]. You have broken my bonds in two. My heart and my tongue will offer to you the sacrifice of praise." Yea, let all my bones say, "O Lord, who is like you?" Let them answer that you are my salvation. Who am I, and what am I? What evil deeds have I not committed, either in deed, words, or intention? But you, O Lord, are good and merciful. Your right hand took notice of the depth of my spiritual death. From the bottom of my heart you have emptied the abyss of my corruption. The result was that I began to will what you willed instead of, as before, doing only what I willed. But where was my free will during all those years? From what deep and secret place did you in a moment call forth my will to receive you freely? How, in a moment, did you submit my neck to your easy yoke and my shoulders to your light burden, O Christ Jesus, my Helper and my Redeemer?

AUGUSTINE, BISHOP OF HIPPO, *CONFESSIONS*, BK. 9, CHAP. 1, SEC. 1

COME THEN, LORD, and help your people,
Bought with the price of your own blood,
And bring us with your saints to glory everlasting.
Save your people, Lord, and bless your inheritance;
Govern and uphold them, now and always.
Day by day we bless you;
We praise your name forever. Amen.

"YOU ARE GOD" AND SUFFRAGE B, DAILY MORNING PRAYER: RITE II, IN BCP

FOR REFLECTION: Pss. 35:10; 51:10-19; 72:18-19; 106:47-48; **116:16-17**; Luke 19:8; Rom. 5:1-5; Gal. 2:20; Eph. 1:15-23; Phil. 2:12-13

63

And what is this God? I asked the earth, "Are you that for which I long?" It answered, "I am not He." Then everything inside the earth gave the same answer. So I asked the sea and its depths, and all creeping things. They answered, "We are not your God; you must seek beyond us." So I asked the moving air above. The air with all his inhabitants answered, "Anaximenes of Miletus, the Greek philosopher who thought the air was the source of all things, was deceived; I am not God." Finally, I turned to the heavens; I asked the heavens, the sun, the moon, and the stars. "Neither," they said, "are we the God whom you seek." So I said to everything I met beyond the door of my flesh, to the whole creation, "You have told me of my God, that you are not he. Then tell me something about God." They all cried with a loud voice, "He made us all!"

Augustine, Bishop of Hippo, *Confessions*, Bk. 10, Chap. 6, Sec. 9

> *Keep us today, Lord, from all sin;*
> *Have mercy on us, Lord, have mercy.*
> *Lord, show us your love and mercy;*
> *For we put our trust in you.*
> *In you, Lord, is our hope;*
> *And we shall never hope in vain. Amen.*
>
> Suffrage B, Daily Morning Prayer: Rite II, in BCP

FOR REFLECTION: Gen. 1:1-26; Neh. 9:6; Pss. 146:6; 148:2-5; Isa. 37:16; Jer. 10:11-16; 40:28; John 1:1-5; 1 Cor. 2:11; 13:12; Rev. 4:11

64

How you have loved us, good Father, who did not spare your only Son, but delivered him up for the ungodly! How you have loved us, for he who thought it not robbery to be equal with you was nevertheless made subject even to death on the cross. He alone, over whom death had no power, had power to lay down his life and power to take it up again. He was, for us to you, both Victor and Victim, the Victor because he was willing to become the Victim. He was, for us to you, Priest and Sacrifice, Priest because of the Sacrifice. By serving us he made us to become your servants, and by new birth made us to be your children. Well then is my hope firmly established in him, that you will through him heal all my infirmities, for he now sits at your right hand and makes intercession for us. Were this not true I would despair. For many and great are my infirmities; but your medicine is stronger. We would have completely despaired, because we would have thought your Word too far removed from us had he not been made flesh of our flesh and dwelt among us.

    AUGUSTINE, BISHOP OF HIPPO, *CONFESSIONS*, BK. 10, CHAP. 43, SEC. 69

SHINE FORTH within our hearts the incorruptible light of Thy knowledge, O Master, Lover of mankind, and open the eyes of our mind to the understanding of . . . Thy Gospel; instill in us also the fear of Thy blessed commandments, that, trampling down all lusts of the flesh, we may pursue a spiritual way of life, being mindful of and doing all that is well-pleasing unto Thee. Amen.

    JOHN CHRYSOSTOM, *THE DIVINE LITURGY OF ST. JOHN CHRYSOSTOM*, ORTHODOX.NET

FOR REFLECTION: Pss. 88:5; 103:3; John 1:14; Rom. 5:8; 8:32-39; 2 Cor. 5:14; 13:14; Gal. 2:20; Phil. 2:6-8

65

There is a major qualitative difference between things temporal and things eternal. A temporal object is valued more before we possess it than afterward; its value begins to fade the moment we possess it. Temporal objects cannot satisfy the soul whose true resting-place is in the eternal. On the other hand, an eternal object is loved more when it is finally obtained than when it is still an object of desire. No one, while longing for the eternal, can value it more highly than it should be. Rather, no matter how great the value someone places on the eternal while on the heavenly journey, when the eternal arrives, its value will continue to increase.

One day sight will displace faith, and hope will be swallowed up in that perfect joy with the Lord at which we will arrive. Our love, on the other hand, will grow stronger even as sight replaces faith and hope. If by faith we love what we do not yet see, how much more will we love when we see? And if we love through hope what we have not yet reached, how much greater will be our love when we reach it?

AUGUSTINE, BISHOP OF HIPPO, ON CHRISTIAN DOCTRINE,
BK. I, CHAP. 38, SEC. 42

O MERCIFUL HEAVENLY FATHER, make me to hunger for you with all my heart and to thirst for you with my inmost being; make me serve only you with all my being. May with all my energies I pursue what is well-pleasing in your sight. And so to you, with Jesus Christ, your only begotten Son and our Lord, and with the Holy Spirit, the Paraclete, your most holy Gift, be all honor and glory forever and ever. Amen.

ANSELM, ARCHBISHOP OF CANTERBURY, BOOK OF MEDITATIONS AND PRAYERS,
MEDITATION 8, SEC. 37

FOR REFLECTION: Rom. 15:13; Gal. 5:5; Eph. 1:18; Col. 1:5, 23, 27; Heb. 12:1-13; 1 Pet. 1:8; 4:1-11; 5:6-11; 2 Pet. 3:14-18

66

"Blessed are the peacemakers, for they shall be called the children of God." By subjecting themselves to reason, and by having their fleshly impulses governed, they constitute a kingdom governed by God. Here things are arranged so that what is of supreme importance reigns unchallenged. The whole is brought under the discipline of what is best, to Truth itself—the only begotten Son of God.

The kingdom's peacemakers will discipline inferior things by what is superior. This is the peace given on earth, and it marks a mature and wise Christian. From such a kingdom, brought to peace and order, the prince of this world has been cast out.

When the peace of the kingdom of God has been inwardly established, the expelled prince of darkness will stir up trouble. The failure of his tactics will expose how carefully and with what strength God's kingdom has been constructed. Hence it follows, "Blessed are they who are persecuted for righteousness' sake, for theirs is the kingdom of heaven."

AUGUSTINE, BISHOP OF HIPPO, OUR LORD'S SERMON ON THE MOUNT,
BK. I, CHAP. 2, SEC. 9

LORD JESUS, you are the Savior of lost sheep, Hope of the exiles, Strength of those who are heavy laden, Repose of the anxious spirit, and Solace and healing Refreshment for the tearful soul that longs for peace. You are the Fountain of all graces, and the glorious Offspring of God, yourself also God. O Lord, now let all things in heaven above and in earth beneath bless you, for you are great, with the Father and Holy Spirit, one God eternal. Amen.

ANSELM, ARCHBISHOP OF CANTERBURY, BOOK OF MEDITATIONS AND PRAYERS,
MEDITATION 9, SEC. 49

FOR REFLECTION: Matt. 5:9-10; 16:17-20; Luke 2:14; 2 Cor. 11:16–12:10; James 3:13-18; 5:7-12; 2 Pet. 4:12-19

JOHN CASSIAN

John Cassian (Johannes Cassianus, ca. AD 360–ca. 435) was born in Scythia Minor, on the Romanian and Bulgarian border. While in early manhood, he journeyed to Bethlehem, where he entered a monastery. There he became a student of Abbot Germanus. In AD 384 the two men, now good friends, made a pilgrimage to the Egyptian hermits. The peaceful solitude made such a profound impression on them they remained among the hermits for seven years. While there, Cassian became a student of Evagrius Ponticus, a classical scholar. On leaving Egypt, Cassian and Germanus made their way to Constantinople, where they became associated with John Chrysostom, patriarch of Constantinople. There John Cassian was consecrated a deacon. His peaceful residency in Constantinople was interrupted when Chrysostom was forced to leave Constantinople because of his perceived support of the theology of Origen of Alexandria. John Cassian was sent to Rome to defend Chrysostom before Pope Innocent I.

While in Rome, John Cassian was invited to establish a monastery in southern Gaul, near Marseilles, on the pattern of the Egyptian monks. Part of the reason John Cassian agreed was that when Alaric sacked Rome (AD 410), John became convinced religious peace and holiness could be obtained only by exiting society. In AD 415 he founded the Abbey of St. Victor. It accommodated men and women monastics, a model for future monasteries in the West.

To instruct his students, Cassian wrote two books. The first book stated the external rules for ordering a hermit's life. In the second book Cassian set forth the internal pattern for finally reaching the monastic goal of holiness. For him, Christian holiness means loving God and one's neighbor with one's whole heart, and the whole person being integrated according to divine love and grace.

John Cassian's *Conferences* provides a glimpse into the lives of the early Christian monastics. From the *Conferences* we learn much about the distinction between authentic and superficial discipleship.

Cassian died at the Abbey of St. Victor ca. AD 435.

67

It happens to some who have supposedly renounced this world—including great wealth—to follow Christ that afterward their peace becomes disturbed over the smallest of things. It might be a knife or pencil. If they had kept their eyes fixed on gaining a pure heart, they would not have allowed their peace to be upset by such trifling things. Some monks guard their books so jealously they will not allow them to be slightly moved or touched. Consequently, they jeopardize their peace with Christ. They should see this as a warning, for they are in danger of being captured by impatience, even spiritual death.

They should concentrate on acquiring patience and love. They claim to have given up everything for the love of Christ. Yet they demonstrate the spirit of their old earthly disposition. The smallest of disturbances unsettle their discipleship. As a result, they become spiritually barren, void of love. The holy life is not achieved simply by self-denial—giving up our goods or casting away our honors. Unless there is love—the true purity of heart—nothing else really matters. Not to be envious, not to be puffed up, not to be angry, not to seek one's own, not to rejoice in iniquity, not to think evil—what is all this but always to offer God a perfect and clean heart and to keep it free from what is contrary to love?

John Cassian, *Conferences*, pt. 1, conference 1 (Abbot Moses), chap. 6

Grant me, O Lord, an upright heart that no perverse intention can lead astray; an unfettered heart that no impetuous desires can enslave. Amen.

Thomas Aquinas, in "Prayers by St. Thomas Aquinas," St. Thomas Prayers

FOR REFLECTION: Luke 15:21-32; 18:18-30; 21:1-4; Rom. 6:1-23; 12:3-21; 1 Cor. 3:16—4:5; 13:1-13

68

Every Christian activity and spiritual practice must have love as its goal. Love with a pure heart is the reason for seeking solitude and practicing fasting, engaging in vigils, reading the Scriptures, and developing Christian virtues. We do these things to prepare ourselves for a pure love to God and neighbor and to keep from being harmed by evil passions. These practices are but aids or steps to the perfection of charity. If for some reason we are prevented from carrying out our customary spiritual disciplines, we should not be defeated by frustration or anger.

What we gain by fasting will not offset what we lose in anger, nor will the value gained by reading the Bible overcome the harm that results from despising our sister or brother. As important as fasting, prayer, vigils, and readings are, they hold secondary importance when compared with our central goal—love with a pure heart. In pursuit of fasting, prayer, and readings let us not drive away the central Christian value. As long as that goal is intact and unharmed, we will not be harmed by the necessary omission of any of these other things. On the other hand, it will be of no value to have done all these other things unless love occupies the primary position.

JOHN CASSIAN, *CONFERENCES*, PT. 1, CONFERENCE 1 (ABBOT MOSES), CHAP. 7

O LORD, give us a mind that is humble, quiet, peaceable, patient, and charitable, and a taste of your Holy Spirit in all our thoughts, words, and deeds.

O Lord, give us a lively faith, a firm hope. . . . Give us fervor and delight in thinking of you, your grace, and your tender compassion toward us. Amen.

THOMAS MORE, "PRAYER FOR FERVOR IN THINKING OF GOD,"
ST. THOMAS PRAYERS

FOR REFLECTION: Matt. 13:1-8, 18-23, 44-45; 18:1-9; Luke 8:16-18; 14:25-34; 18:9-14; 1 Cor. 13:1-13; James 4:1-10

69

A craftsman is anxious to obtain the tools he needs for his work. But they are not ends in themselves. They are used to practice his craft and therefore play an auxiliary role. A person who would simply be content to own the tools as the highest value in themselves—no matter how well made they might be—and doesn't know how to use them is ignorant indeed.

In the same way, fastings, vigils, meditation on the Scriptures, self-denial, and abandonment of one's possessions do not themselves constitute a holy life; they are but aids to a holy life, tools for pursuing Christian holiness. A Christian engages in these practices to no profit if he thinks that they constitute a holy life and fails to place them in service to love made perfect. He owns the implements of holiness but is ignorant of their purpose.

Whatever can disturb purity of heart and peace of mind—even though it may seem useful—should be avoided. By this rule we shall make straight for holy love.

JOHN CASSIAN, *CONFERENCES*, PT. 1, CONFERENCE 1 (ABBOT MOSES), CHAP. 7

GRANT, O LORD, I beseech you, that I may be drawn to you. Draw this whole self of mine, O Lord, into your love. All that I am is yours by creation; make all of it yours by love. Behold, O Lord, my heart lies open before you. You who have caused me to seek you, cause me to receive you. Cling to him, O my soul; cling, cling with insistent desire. Amen.

ANSELM, ARCHBISHOP OF CANTERBURY, *MEDITATIONS AND PRAYERS*, MEDITATION 11, SEC. 54

FOR REFLECTION: Matt. 23:3-19; Luke 6:43-49; 2 Tim. 3:5; Titus 1:15-16; Rev. 2:1-7; 3:7-13, 19-22

70

Contemplation of God happens in many ways. Not only do we see God when we worship the Trinity, but we also see God through the greatness of his creation, his just ways, and his daily providence. We see God when with pure minds we contemplate what he has done for his people in every generation and when with trembling hearts we admire the majesty with which he directs and governs all things.

We can see God when we realize all our days, hours, and the ages past and future are known to him.

Best of all, we see God when we gaze in unmeasured admiration on his incomprehensible mercy. With unwearied patience he endures the countless sins being committed under his very eyes. When there were no prior merits of our own, through grace alone God made himself known to us. Then by the free grace of his pity he reconciled us to himself. God is revealed in the numberless opportunities for salvation extended to us. Indeed, from our cradles he has extended his grace and knowledge of his law.

JOHN CASSIAN, *CONFERENCES*, PT. 1, CONFERENCE 1 (ABBOT MOSES), CHAP. 15

O LORD MY GOD, teach me to be obedient without reserve, poor without servility, chaste without compromise, humble without being pretentious, joyful without being lustful, serious without trying to impress others, active without frivolity, submissive without bitterness, truthful without deceit, fruitful in good works without being self-congratulatory, quick to help my neighbor without arrogance, and quick to edify others by word and example without being dishonest. Amen.

THOMAS AQUINAS, "A PRAYER BY THOMAS AQUINAS," ST. THOMAS PRAYERS

FOR REFLECTION: Pss. 25:1-11; 33:18-22; 94:17-19; Isa. 55:1-13; Matt. 18:21-35; Luke 1:46-53; Rom. 3:21-31; 5:1-11; Eph. 2:1-10; Heb. 4:14-16; 1 Pet. 2:9-12

71

The waterwheel used for grinding grain can teach us how to treat unwanted thoughts. Water rushes over the waterwheel and makes the wheel turn. The wheel does not stop as long as water runs over it. However, the miller can decide what grain he loads into the millstone. Will it be wheat, barley, or weeds?

In the same manner, torrents of wayward thoughts, temptations, and trials tumble over our minds and set them spinning. We can no more escape them than a waterwheel can escape turning. However, a person of character can determine which thoughts will be entertained and which to cast away. But this requires diligence similar to that of the miller. A Christian must discipline his or her mind through prayer, through meditation on the Holy Scriptures, and by planting the things of the Holy Spirit in one's memory. There must be a commitment to holiness in all parts of our lives.

If we permit ourselves to be overcome by sloth or carelessness, if we spend our time in idle gossip, permit ourselves to be entangled in the cares of this world, or become overwhelmed by unnecessary anxiety, then tares will spring up in our hearts.

JOHN CASSIAN, *CONFERENCES*, PT. 1, CONFERENCE 1 (ABBOT MOSES), CHAP. 18

O TRIUNE GOD, what a sure foundation for joy if by your Spirit we make it our goal to be completely possessed by you, if our wills are transformed into your will, and if our greatest desire is to be pleasing to you. Through the ministry of the Holy Spirit, let me offer myself to you as a living sacrifice. Amen.

HENRY SCOUGAL, *THE LIFE OF GOD IN THE SOUL OF MAN*, PT. 2

FOR REFLECTION: Prov. 25:28; Matt. 5:13-16; 6:19-21; 7:1-5; 1 Cor. 2:12; 9:24-27; 2 Cor. 4:7-12; Eph. 5:8-11; 6:10-18; 2 Tim. 2:1-4; Titus 2:11-14

72

The power of discernment is fourfold. *First* is the ability to distinguish between authentic and vacuous values. People treat some things as gold when they are only painted that way to distract from the truly valuable. The *second* is the ability to distinguish between works of true righteousness and those like counterfeit coins. They bear the king's image but on inspection are discovered to be falsely stamped. We must learn to distinguish between teaching that is heretical and teaching that bears the gold standard of Scripture. The *third* power of discernment is to recognize those whose true weight and value are nothing more than the rust of vanity. Vanity weighs nothing on the scales of the apostles and fathers. When we do anything to gain human glory, we are just laying up treasure on earth where rust and moth corrupt. The powers of evil will destroy such "treasure," and moths of pride will consume it. *Fourth,* we must regularly search the inner rooms of our hearts. Examine the footsteps of all who enter. Otherwise, some beast might pass through and then show others the entrance. Daily, we must use the gospel plow to turn up the soil of our hearts. Then we can know if an intruder has entered.

JOHN CASSIAN, *CONFERENCES*, PT. 1, CONFERENCE 1 (ABBOT MOSES), CHAP. 22

O MY ALL-MERCIFUL GOD AND LORD, Jesus Christ, full of pity: Through your great love you descended from your throne and became incarnate in order to save the human race. O Savior, I beseech you to save me by your grace! . . . Let faith and not my unworthy works be counted to me, O my God. Amen.

FROM A PRAYER BY JOHN CHRYSOSTOM, "SEASONAL PRAYERS: FOR LENT," PRAYERS, IBREVIARY.COM

FOR REFLECTION: Ps. 39:1-24; Prov. 1:1-33; **Matt. 6:19-21**; Acts 20:28-31; Rom. 12:3; 16:17-18; 2 Cor. 13:5; Gal. 1:8-10; 6:3-5; Phil. 1:10; James 1:22-25

73

In the history of the church there have been many shipwrecks because people failed to obtain and practice the grace of discernment. Christian discretion is not a virtue one gains in his own strength. True Christian discernment comes by aid of the Holy Spirit. The apostle Paul counts it as one of the Spirit's noblest gifts. He emphasizes that the gift of discernment is no small matter. It is a prize of divine grace that must be carefully developed. Otherwise, ill spirits will surely arise in us and lead us astray. In the darkness we will fall into dangerous pits and cliffs and err in matters that should be plain and straightforward.

Without discernment the most vigorous Christian disciplines—fasting, vigils, solitude, self-denials, duties of kindness—will be brought to a terrible end. Discretion, born of the Holy Spirit, permits us to walk along the road and avoid excesses on either side—being puffed up by zeal and virtue, on one side, and lukewarmness and vices, on the other. Did not our Lord tell us that "if your eyes are good, your whole body will be full of light"? But failure to be discerning will darken our spiritual vision and actions.

JOHN CASSIAN, *CONFERENCES*, PT. I, CONFERENCE 2 (ABBOT MOSES), CHAPS. I-2

HOLY SPIRIT, POWERFUL COUNSELOR, sacred Bond of the Father and the Son, we believe that when you dwell in us, you also prepare a dwelling for the Father and the Son. Let no evil desire take possession of me. Come to me, Glory of the living and Hope of the dying. Lead me by your grace that I may always be pleasing to you. Amen.

ATTRIBUTED TO AUGUSTINE, BISHOP OF HIPPO, "PRAYER FOR THE INDWELLING OF THE HOLY SPIRIT," *THE FRESH ANOINTING*

FOR REFLECTION: 1 Kings 3:9; Prov. 2:1-5; 23:1-2; **Matt. 6:19-24**; 1 Cor. 12:8-11; 2 Cor. 11:13-15; Phil. 1:9-10; Col. 2:8; 1 John 4:1-6

74

Why would David ask God for insight into his commandments? He knew the law. And nature had given him an ability to think well. What more did he need? The answer is that by using nothing more than human wisdom a person cannot comprehend the way of the Lord. Daily the Lord must illumine him. Claiming nothing of merit for himself, David knew God's enabling grace alone makes true understanding and obedience possible.

The apostle Paul also knew this. He said God must enable us to will God's will. Our will, and its good execution, must be set free by the Lord. Moreover, the very beginning of our conversion, our expression of faith, and the endurance of sufferings are the Lord's gracious gifts.

It is not enough that the beginning of salvation is by grace; only by grace does redemption continue and reach completion. The Lord alone lifts up the fallen, makes the foolish wise, and gives victory to those defeated by sin.

None of this dismisses the importance of our wills, our efforts, or our zeal. But it teaches us that we cannot move toward the Lord unless first he graciously moves toward us. Nor can our efforts procure a pure heart unless first it is granted by God's grace and power.

JOHN CASSIAN, *Conferences*, PT. 1, CONFERENCE 3 (ABBOT PAPHNUTIUS), CHAP. 15

O Lord my God, I could not have begun to love you had you not first begun to love me. I well know that for me "death and condemnation deserved" were written on the gates of hell, but because of your inestimable love, "free gift of grace" has been written on the gate of heaven. Hallelujah! Amen.

FOR REFLECTION: 1 Sam. 2:9; Pss. 68:28; 118:14; 119:124-25; 146:5-9; Prov. 21:31; 2 Cor. 3:5-6; Phil. 1:29; 2:13; 3:7-16; Heb. 2:1-4; 10:19-26

75

So thoroughly did the apostles realize that everything regarding our salvation comes from the gracious Lord that they even asked that faith be granted to them. They had no expectation that the human will can generate faith. They knew all trust in the Lord must be given by God as a free gift. The Lord himself is the Author of our salvation. He teaches us how feeble, weak, and insufficient humanly generated faith would be. Faith must come as a gift from the Lord, and it must be constantly strengthened by him. Jesus told Peter, "Simon, Simon, behold, Satan has desired to have you that he may sift you as wheat. But I have prayed to my Father that your faith fail not." When Peter's feeble faith was being lashed by waves of unbelief, imminently threatened by shipwreck, he cried out, "Lord, help my unbelief."

JOHN CASSIAN, *CONFERENCES*, PT. 1, CONFERENCE 3 (ABBOT PAPHNUTIUS), CHAP. 16

LET US THEN BESEECH GOD and believe in love and much hope that he may give us the heavenly grace of the Spirit and that the Spirit himself may govern and guide us into the perfect will of God and refresh us in all the variety of his refreshing. Amen.

MACARIUS-SYMEON, *FIFTY SPIRITUAL HOMILIES*, HOMILY 18, SEC. 10

FOR REFLECTION: Matt. 8:23-27; **14:22-23**; **Mark 9:22-24**; **Luke 17:5**; **22:31-32**; John 1:17; 6:65; 15:4-5; Rom. 5:8; 10:1; 1 Cor. 4:7; Eph. 2:8-9; Heb. 11:1-2

76

Many who say they have renounced the world to become monks wear a monk's garb, but everything else about them remains the same. They lust for wealth, disguise their lust as a commitment to holiness, and label hoarding as preparation for ministering to the needy.

If they were truly pursuing a holy life, they would strip themselves of their old sinful selves. They would place themselves under disciplines that lead to holiness. They are eager to rule over others but are unwilling for anyone to govern them. They insist on teaching others but are unwilling to be taught. They are "blind leaders of the blind."

First, they present themselves as humble and serious Christians. *Second,* they are determined to show they are inferior to no one. They act as if they are better informed than anyone. They often break out into ill-informed and ill-considered speech.

Sins hidden under the guise of virtue and traveling in the costume of holiness are worse and more difficult to alter than a life openly committed to carnal pleasures. The latter can be confronted and cured. The former causes their victims to descend deeper into danger and death.

JOHN CASSIAN, *CONFERENCES*, PT. 1, CONFERENCE 4 (ABBOT DANIEL), CHAP. 20

O SOVEREIGN AND ALMIGHTY GOD, whatever sin we commit, in your goodness and mercy be pleased to pardon. Leave us not, O Lord, while we hope in you, nor lead us into temptation, but deliver us from the evil one and from his works, through the grace, mercy, and love of your only begotten Son. Amen.

THE DIVINE LITURGY OF THE HOLY APOSTLE AND EVANGELIST MARK (BEFORE AD 200)

FOR REFLECTION: Matt. 15:13-14; Rom. 6:19; Eph. 4:17-32; 1 Thess. 3:8-13; 2 Tim. 3:5; James 1:8; 1 John 1:4-10; Jude vv. 12-13; Rev. 3:14-18

77

There is an enormous difference between one who tries to extinguish the fire of sin through fear of hell and a desire for future rewards and one who has a horror of sin and its uncleanness. The latter is motivated by love for God. He takes hold of purity and virtue because he longs for holiness. Motivated by love, he needs no promise of future rewards. He simply rejoices in the good things of the Lord. He delights in virtue in and of itself, not because it is a way to escape punishment. Moved by God's love, in the absence of those who watch him, he does not act on an opportunity to sin. Neither will he secretly permit himself to be enticed by evil thoughts. In the marrow of his soul there resides a love for godliness that bars sin's entrance and hates it passionately.

By contrast, when reasons for avoiding evil are removed from one who serves God only to escape punishment, he will return to what he loves. Acquaintance with what is good ceases. Being a stranger to purity, such a person will never know the peace of God.

The person who knows the peace of the Lord, and who loves godliness for its own sake, will forever comply with what is good, for his love is free of all deceit.

JOHN CASSIAN, *CONFERENCES*, PT. 2, CONFERENCE 11 (ABBOT CHAEREMON), CHAP. 8

O ETERNAL FATHER, by the indwelling Holy Spirit, make our love for you to abound yet more and more in knowledge and depth of insight. Enlighten us so that we may discern the things that are excellent and that we may be filled with the unalloyed fruit of righteousness that comes through Jesus Christ, to the glory and praise of God. Amen.

FOR REFLECTION: Matt. 8:5-14, 24-27; 13:4-45; Luke 11:37-54; John 12:42-50; 14:15-24; 2 Cor. 5:13-19; Col. 2:1-4

78

There is a qualitative difference between one who serves God as his child and someone who is only a servant. The child serves the Father in love; the servant, out of fear and a mercenary desire for rewards. The child seeks the Father's glory; but everything the servant does is for selfish gain.

By adoption, God wants to transform servants into sons and daughters who serve him with enduring love. He wants his children to be formed in his image, to delight in his goodness because he is their Father. Like their Father, they will share his longing to reconcile sinners and make them God's children.

God's children will show others his gentleness and patience. They will recall how they were poisoned by passions before the Father healed them. They will recall how they became the children of God through grace alone. Had not the Lord helped them, their souls would have dwelt in hell. In like manner, God's children must love their enemies, must do good to those who hate them, and must pray for their persecutors. Then God's children will be godlike and recognized as his children.

How can a weak and fragile human be like God? Only by imitating him, by showing a calm love for all people.

JOHN CASSIAN, *CONFERENCES*, PT. 2, CONFERENCE 11 (ABBOT CHAEREMON), CHAP. 9

YOU, CHILDREN, praise the Lord; praise the name of the Lord. We praise you, we sing hymns to you, we bless you for your great glory, O Lord our King, the Father of Christ the immaculate Lamb, who takes away the sin of the world. Amen.

"DAILY PRAYERS," IN *CONSTITUTIONS OF THE HOLY APOSTLES*, BK. 7, SEC. 5.48

FOR REFLECTION: Ps. 16:9-11; Matt. 5:1-16, 38-48; 6:5-13; 18:10-14, 21-25; Luke 12:47; Rom. 8:5-11; Gal. 3:26-29; Col. 2:13; 1 John 1:8, 10; 3:1-3, 9-10; 4:17; 5:18

79

When a Christian has acquired the love for God, when he seeks to be formed by the holiness of God, he will be endowed with the Lord's heart of compassion. He will pray for those who persecute him, as Jesus did on the cross: "Father, forgive them, for they know not what they do."

When a Christian is unwilling to show sorrow over the sins of others, that is a sure sign that he has not yet been purged from sin's pollution. If a Christian insists on retaining the disposition of a censorious judge, how does he expect to obtain Christian holiness? He lacks the very thing the apostle said we must practice if we expect to do God's will: "Bear one another's burdens and so fulfill the law of Christ." If a person has not the virtue of love that is kind, rejoices in the truth, not envious, not boastful, not arrogant or rude, how can he claim to be formed in the Father's image?

JOHN CASSIAN, *CONFERENCES*, PT. 2, CONFERENCE 11 (ABBOT CHAEREMON), CHAP. 10

LORD, make us instruments of your peace. Where there is hatred, let us sow love; where there is injury, pardon; where there is discord, union; where there is doubt, faith; where there is despair, hope; where there is darkness, light; where there is sadness, joy. Grant that we may not so much seek to be consoled as to console; to be understood as to understand; to be loved as to love. For it is in giving that we receive; it is in pardoning that we are pardoned; and it is in dying that we are born to eternal life. Amen.

"A PRAYER ATTRIBUTED TO ST. FRANCIS," PRAYERS AND THANKSGIVINGS, IN BCP

FOR REFLECTION: Ps. 116:16-17; Prov. 12:10; 13:17; Mal. 1:6; Matt. 5:43-48; **Luke** 6:27-36; 12:47; 18; **23:34**; 1 Cor. 13:4-7; **Gal. 6:2**; 1 Pet. 1:8; 1 John 1:8-10; 3:9; 4:17; 5:16-18

VINCENT OF LÉRINS

From the beginning there have been innumerable opportunities for the clear stream of the Christian faith to be diverted into shallows that would trap it in pools inhabited by insects, moss, and algae. Every potential diversion has offered itself as the proper direction for the faith. How may the church distinguish between the "faith that was once for all entrusted to the saints" (Jude v. 3, NRSV) and unending perversions of the "grace of our God" (v. 4, NRSV)?

That question was addressed and answered directly by a fifth-century monk of the monastery of Lérins, located on an island about a mile offshore from the French Riviera town of Cannes. He wrote under the pseudonym of Peregrinus. In AD 434, Vincent of Lérins (d. ca. AD 445) asked and answered our question in his *Commonitory* (letter of instruction).

The *Commonitory* contains thirty-three chapters. It was written to help keep Vincent's belief in line with the teachings of the church fathers. He observed that a teacher's doctrinal error is the "people's trial," a trial that becomes more perilous in proportion to the errant teacher's learning (chap. 17, sec. 42). A second *Commonitory* was written, but we do not possess it.

Eucherius (d. ca. AD 449), bishop of Lyon, called Vincent a holy person who was conspicuous for his eloquence and knowledge. Vincent's norm for distinguishing between true and false doctrine has made its way into the standard vocabulary of the church.

80

I have asked many saintly and learned persons for a universal standard for distinguishing between the true Christian faith and doctrinal error. Almost always the answers have been that anyone who wishes to be sound in their faith and detect false teachers can with God's help fortify their faith. *First,* test all doctrine by the authority of Scripture. *Second,* test what is taught against the church's doctrinal heritage.

But if Scripture is a complete and sufficient standard for Christian doctrine, why appeal to the church's doctrinal tradition? Because of the depth and diversity of the Scriptures, they are interpreted in many different ways and seem to yield as many interpretations as there are interpreters. False teachers always appeal to the Bible. Therefore, because of so many interpretations and heresies, the rule for a right understanding of Scripture and for deciding true Christian doctrine relies on the tradition of the church as found in its creeds and general councils.

This yields the following rule: only the faith the church throughout its history has affirmed *everywhere*, *always*, and *by all* should be received as true—*universality, antiquity,* and *common consent.* This is the "catholic" faith. We observe *universality* if we believe only what the church throughout the world confesses; *antiquity* if we embrace the apostles' and fathers' teachings; and *consent* if we accept only the creeds and councils the church affirms.

VINCENT OF LÉRINS, *COMMONITORY*, CHAP. 2, SECS. 4-6

BY BLESSING THOSE THAT BLESS YOU, O Lord, and sanctifying those that trust in you, save your people and preserve the fullness of your church. Amen.

JOHN CHRYSOSTOM, IN *THE DIVINE LITURGY OF ST. JOHN CHRYSOSTOMOS*,
THE ORTHODOX CHRISTIAN PAGE

FOR REFLECTION: Matt. 7:15-23; John 8:48-59; 16:13-14; Gal. 1:6-10; Eph. 4:1-5; Phil. 2:5-11; Col. 1:15-23; 1 Tim. 1:3-5; 6:20; 2 Tim. 4:1-5; 1 John 4:1-6

81

Troublemakers bearing their self-serving distortion of the gospel found their way to Galatia. When Christians there heard false teachers spewing out errors, many swallowed the garbage without question. Paul sternly exercised his apostolic office and told the straying Galatians, "If we, or an angel from heaven, preach any other gospel to you than that which we have preached to you, let him be accursed." Why did Paul say "if we" instead of "if I"? Because he meant that even if any other apostles were to preach a gospel different from what they had received from Christ, they should be accursed. To preserve unadulterated the faith once delivered, Paul spares no one, and he doesn't stop with the apostles. "If an angel from heaven preach any other gospel to you than that which we have preached to you, let him be accursed." That is how inviolable the gospel is. Let anyone who subverts the faith of one of the Lord's sheep be quickly excluded, lest the deadly disease spread to all.

Preaching a distorted faith was deceitful in the past, and it will be deceitful in the future. To protect the church by excluding those who preach something other than the pure gospel is the church's unrelenting responsibility. Today, Paul cries out, "If anyone preaches any new doctrine, let him be accursed."

VINCENT OF LÉRINS, *COMMONITORY*, CHAP. 8, SECS. 21-23;
CHAP. 9, SECS. 25-26

I LOVE YOUR KINGDOM, LORD,
The house of your abode,
The church our blest Redeemer saved
With his own precious blood. Amen.

TIMOTHY DWIGHT (1752–1817), HYMNARY

✛ ✛ ✛

FOR REFLECTION: Matt. 7:15-23; 1 Cor. 1:18-31; 2 Cor. 4:1-18; 5:11-21; 12:2; **Gal. 1:6-10**; 5:16; Rev. 22:10-17

82

There is always a danger we will think of the Word of God as having assumed human nature merely in appearance, not as truly human. We must not think of Christ as if he were an actor who puts on a mask and plays the role of another. The actor plays the role of a priest or a king but is not in fact a real priest or king. The play ends; the character the actor represented ceases to be; the actor resumes his former "self."

That is not what the incarnation means. We must never accept such a misrepresentation. The Lord is no actor. In reality the Word of God took on himself our full humanity. He lived a human life, not as merely imitating humans, but as the very flesh-and-blood Jesus of Nazareth. Having become human as we are, Jesus spoke, acted, and suffered, yet without jeopardizing his deity.

Away with all notions that our Lord can't fully identify with us! Let us rejoice that while Christ remained fully God, he took on himself all it means to be human. And after his passion, he did not "escape" as an actor does when a play has ended. No, as our Mediator in heaven he permanently bears his humanity and ours.

VINCENT OF LÉRINS, *COMMONITORY*, CHAP. 14, SECS. 38-39

> *O GOD,*
> *I bind this day to me forever,*
> *By power of faith, Christ's incarnation. Amen.*
> PATRICK (CA. AD 387–CA. 463), TRANS. CECIL F. ALEXANDER (1889),
> HYMNARY

FOR REFLECTION: Isa. 51:1-2; Matt. 1:18-23; 4:2; 26:23-46; Luke 2:1-40; 23:26-56; John 1:1-14; 4:6; Phil. 2:5-11; Heb. 5:7-10; 1 John 1:1-4; 2 John vv. 7-11

83

He is the true and genuine catholic Christian who loves the truth of God, loves the body of Christ, values the Christian faith above all earthly authorities and above the favor, brilliance, eloquence, and philosophy of any human. He attaches relatively little importance to any of these and continues steadfastly established in the faith. He resolves that he will believe only that which he is sure the catholic faith has held universally and from antiquity.

Whatever novel and formerly unheard-of doctrine he finds to have been deceitfully introduced, he will judge as an opponent of true Christian faith. Anything that is contrary to what the apostles, fathers, and saints have believed will be seen as nothing more than a test of the church's fidelity to Christ. The true catholic Christian will be instructed by the apostle Paul: "There must be heresies so that those who are approved may be made known among you." It is as though Paul had said, "This is why heresies show up in the church: by rooting out errors, those who are faithful will be revealed." Our tenacity and faithfulness will manifest our abiding love for the Christian faith.

VINCENT OF LÉRINS, *COMMONITORY*, CHAP. 20, SEC. 48

WE PRAY AND BESEECH YOU, O Lover of all people, O good Lord, remember in your good mercy your church throughout the world and all your people. Grant to us the peace of heaven; grant us also the peace of this life. May we be yours, O Lord, for we know no other God but you and name no other name but yours. Give us life, and let no deadly sin prevail against us. For you are the One who blesses and sanctifies all things. To you we ascribe glory and thanksgiving. Amen.

THE DIVINE LITURGY OF THE HOLY APOSTLE AND EVANGELIST MARK
(BEFORE AD 200)

FOR REFLECTION: John 17:6-26; **1 Cor. 11:17-22**; Eph. 4:1–5:21; Rev. 2:1–3:22

84

Each time a novel and false teaching appears in the church, it offers opportunity to distinguish between wheat and chaff. Chaff has no weight to keep it on the threshing floor. It is soon permanently blown away.

Even some of the wheat is severely blown about. There are heretics like this. Although they believe much of what the church teaches, they have embraced notions that are nothing but chaff. O wretched condition. Laden with error, they are afraid of perishing. Wounded and half alive, they are ashamed to return. They have swallowed more poison than they can regurgitate but not enough to kill them. They neither thrive nor die.

They come in two types. The first type is hurled wherever the wind drives it because it adheres to unstable doctrines. A second type blows back on itself like returning waves. Frightened by true doctrine and plagued by doubt, they know not where to turn, what to keep, and what to throw away.

Sitting outside the secure harbor of biblical and apostolic faith, these storm-tossed vessels have almost been destroyed. They have unfurled their sails against the destructive blasts of doctrinal novelty. However, in his compassion God has provided medicine to heal their afflictions if they return to the safe and peaceful harbor, the body of Christ.

Vincent of Lérins, *Commonitory*, chap. 20, secs. 49-50

Turn us, O God of Hosts, show us your countenance, and we shall be whole. For wherever the soul of man turns itself, unless toward you, it is riveted on sorrows even if it is riveted on beautiful things that will pass away. Amen.

Augustine, Bishop of Hippo, *Confessions*, bk. 4, chap. 10, sec. 15

FOR REFLECTION: Matt. 7:15-23; 13:24-35; Rom. 14:1–15:13; 1 Cor. 2:10-17; 12:12-31; Heb. 6:19; 1 Pet. 1:3

85

The church is the careful and watchful guardian of the doctrines deposited to her charge. At the close of the New Testament era, Christian doctrine had not reached its full development. Since then, important doctrinal growth, consistent with the New Testament, has occurred in the body of Christ.

In humans, knowledge and wisdom normally increase. Through the years our bodies and minds develop and reach maturity. But even though stature and outward appearance change, a person's essential nature and identity remain. The adult was latent in the child.

All of this is true of growth in the church. If because of human growth a person were to become another creature, the result would be major distortion. Growth in Christian doctrine and individual discipleship must follow the same laws of progress we see in humans. The church consolidates the early foundations of its faith; this faith is enlarged by time, refined by age, and yet remains uncorrupted, complete, and balanced in all its parts.

VINCENT OF LÉRINS, COMMONITORY, CHAP. 23, SECS. 54-59

> *My Lord, I know not what I ought to ask of you.*
> *You and you alone know my needs.*
> *You love me more than I am able to love you.*
> *O Father, grant to me, your servant, all that I cannot ask.*
> *For a cross I dare not ask, nor for consolation;*
> *I dare only to stand in your presence.*
> *My heart is open to you. Amen.*

"PRAYER OF PHILARET, METROPOLITAN OF MOSCOW," IN *THE ORTHODOX PRAYERS*

FOR REFLECTION: Ps. 92:12-14; Matt. 13:31-35; Rom. 15:13; 1 Cor. 15:28; 2 Cor. 9:6-11; Phil. 1:3-11; 2 Thess. 1:1-12; 2 Tim. 3:19; 4:1-5; Titus 2:1, 11-15; 2 Pet. 3:14-18

86

Let the church of Christ, and we who are its children, be ever watchful guardians of the doctrines deposited to our charge. May we never change anything in them, never diminish them, never amputate what is essential, and never add anything superficial. While dealing faithfully and judiciously with ancient doctrine, let the church carefully keep one object in mind. If antiquity has left anything shapeless and rudimentary, let us fashion and polish it. If it has already been fashioned and polished, then let us strengthen it. If anything has already been ratified and defined, then let us carefully protect it.

In their decisions, the general councils have always sought to state with greater clarity what was earlier believed by clear implication. They have always worked to make our Christian witness more articulate. What might have been earlier preached in essence must now be preached and practiced with even clearer conviction and diligent attention. This is what the "catholic" church, alarmed by the novelties of heretics, has accomplished in the general councils. In its creeds and writings the church has bequeathed to us only what has been received from the apostles and fathers. Often an old article of faith has received a better name for what has always been believed.

VINCENT OF LÉRINS, *COMMONITORY*, CHAP. 23, SECS. 54-59

GRACIOUS FATHER, we pray for your holy catholic church. Fill it with all truth, in all truth with all peace. Where it is corrupt, purify it; where it is in error, direct it; where in anything it is amiss, reform it. Where it is right, strengthen it; where it is in want, provide for it; where it is divided, reunite it; for the sake of Jesus Christ your Son our Savior. Amen.

"FOR THE CHURCH," PRAYERS AND THANKSGIVINGS, IN BCP

FOR REFLECTION: John 8:12-30; Acts 15:35; 1 Cor. 1:18–2:16; Col. 1:15-23; 1 John 4:1-6

LEO THE GREAT

If we expect God to provide church leaders who can match the times, we need look no further than Leo the Great (Pope Leo I, ca. AD 400–461) for confirmation. Next to Gregory the Great, Leo's papal service is the most significant of the ancient church. He cemented the primacy of the bishop of Rome over the whole church. He used his position to ensure orthodoxy and, not always graciously, to establish order. His magnitude was such that he is one of two popes given the epithet "the Great." He was the first great Latin-speaking pope and the first great Italian theologian. In spite of the social and theological crises thrust on him, he was able to produce a rich body of enduring pastoral and spiritual counsel.

We know nothing of Leo's parentage and childhood. Tradition has it that he was born in a town in the north of Etruria (central Italy).

In AD 440 Pope Sixtus III (pope from 432 to 440) sent Leo to mediate between two feuding generals. While on that mission, Sixtus died. Quickly, the people and clergy elected Leo as pope. He served during a period of theological error and social erosion; the empire and paganism were expiring. Not only did heavy ecclesiastical responsibilities rest on him, but Leo also had to fill the role of a civil governor and mediator. He supervised the distribution of grain and reorganized Rome's fire department. When Attila the Hun invaded Italy (AD 452), Leo convinced him to withdraw. And when Gaiseric, the Vandal, took Rome (AD 455), Leo averted the city's complete destruction.

Leo played a significant role in battling Pelagianism and Manichaeism, which denied the Father of Christ is also Creator. Perhaps his most important theological struggle was against Eutyches, who denied the incarnate Christ was of two complete natures—divine and human—in one undivided person. In his *Tome* (AD 449) Leo affirmed the two complete natures and set the stage for the Council of Chalcedon (AD 451), where his position was largely adopted. "In the whole and perfect nature of true man was true God born, complete in what was his own, complete in what was ours" (*Letters*, letter 28, sec. 3).

87

Purged from wicked superstitions, and living in the tradition of the apostles, the fathers gave themselves to deeds of mercy. The sacred value of their example was true of the past and should shape the present and the future. They ministered to the poor, cared for the weak, and did to others as they would have others do to them. The fathers knew that not only are our spiritual riches gifts from God but our earthly possessions also proceed from his bounty. God has not so much given us material possessions as he has made us their temporary stewards. Therefore, he is justified in requiring an account from us. We must use God's gifts wisely. We, too, must give ourselves to deeds of mercy.

Wealth can be of great advantage to society when in the hands of the benevolent and openhanded. So the wealthy person must not squander what God has given, and the miser must not hoard it. It matters not whether what God has given is spent carelessly or selfishly stored; it is equally wasted.

LEO THE GREAT, "ON THE COLLECTIONS, V," *SERMONS*, SERMON 10, SEC. 1

O LORD JESUS CHRIST, we the recipients of your redemption name you our merciful Lord, our great King, our good Shepherd, our Teacher of truth, our seasonable Help, our living Bread, our Priest forever, our true Light, our straight Pathway, our Wisdom and Illumination, our Reconciliation, our safe Protection, our everlasting Salvation, our great Compassion, our unfailing Hope, our perfect Love, our holy Resurrection, and our eternal Life. Mindful of all your benefits, we give thanks to you; we praise and worship you, who with the Father and the Spirit are one God eternally gracious. Amen.

ANSELM, ARCHBISHOP OF CANTERBURY, *BOOK OF MEDITATIONS AND PRAYERS*, MEDITATION 18, SEC. 90

FOR REFLECTION: Luke 12:35-38, 42; 16:1-8; 1 Cor. 12:4-11; Eph. 4:7-13; 1 Tim. 6:17-19; James 1:16-18; 1 Pet. 4:7-11

88

Some rich people may say that although they don't generously minister to the poor, they do many other righteous things and so will surely be excused for lacking this one virtue. They are wrong. Although many other righteous deeds are done, without mercy shown to the dispossessed, nothing else counts. Although a person is full of faith, is sexually pure, and is sober, unless he is merciful, he cannot expect to receive God's mercy.

When the Son of Man comes in his majesty and is seated on his glorious throne, when the nations are gathered before him, and he divides between the righteous and the unrighteous, for what will the righteous be praised except for works of benevolence and deeds of love? Christ will reckon these things as having been done to himself. When in the incarnation Christ made human nature his own, he joined himself to human humility, not to human wealth. On the day of judgment, for what will the unrighteous be judged except for their neglect of love, their refusal to show mercy to the poor? Because of largehearted liberality, Christ will admit many to God's kingdom, while for ungodly insensitivity, he will condemn many to eternal punishment.

Leo the Great, "On the Collections, V," *Sermons*, sermon 10, sec. 3

O Lord Jesus Christ, who seeks those who stray and welcomes them when they return, help me to approach you by frequently hearing your Word, lest I sin against my neighbor by the blindness of human judgment, the harshness of false justice, by considering him unworthy of your grace and placing sinful trust in my own righteousness, or because of my ignorance of divine wisdom. Amen.

"A Prayer from St. Albert the Great on Conscience,"
A Blog for Dallas Area Catholics

✛✛✛

FOR REFLECTION: Matt. 5:7; 7:21-23; 25:31-46; Luke 16:19-31; Rom. 15:7-9; James 2:1-13; 5:1-6

89

If we correctly comprehend the creation, we will understand humans were made in God's image for the purpose of imitating him. We will see that we attain our highest dignity when divine goodness is reflected in us. To that end the Savior's grace is restoring us daily. That which fell in the first Adam is now being lifted up in the second Adam. God's mercy is the cause of this great restoration. We would never have loved God unless he had first loved us and dispelled our darkness. The Lord foretold this through Isaiah: "I will bring the blind into a way they did not know. I will turn darkness into light for them and the crooked into the straight."

Through love, God creates in us the image of his goodness and gives all we need to manifest his goodness. He kindles the lamps of our minds and inflames us with the fire of his love so that we may not only love God but all that he loves. If between humans there can exist a lasting friendship based on similarity of character, we ought to diverge from nothing that pleases God.

LEO THE GREAT, "ON THE FAST OF THE TENTH MONTH, I,"
SERMONS, SERMON 12, SEC. 1

O SOVEREIGN LORD, who chose the lamp of the twelve apostles and sent them forth to proclaim the gospel of your kingdom throughout the world and to heal sickness and every weakness among the people, purify our lives and cleanse our hearts from all pollution and from all wickedness, that with pure heart and conscience we may be to you a sweet savor, through the grace, mercy, and love of your only begotten Son. Amen.

THE DIVINE LITURGY OF THE HOLY APOSTLE AND EVANGELIST MARK
(BEFORE AD 200)

FOR REFLECTION: Ps. 30:5; Isa. 42:16; 65:1; John 10:1-18; 14:15-27; Rom. 5:12-21; 1 Pet. 1:13-25; 1 John 4:7-10, 19; 5:18-20

90

As God's children, let us put on the unfading love of our Author and Ruler. Let us completely subject ourselves to him in whose works and judgments true justice and tenderhearted compassion never fail. This is love made perfect.

However godly we may be, love cannot be made perfect in us unless we love our neighbor. But who is my neighbor? Not only those who are connected by friendship or neighborhood, but absolutely all persons with whom we share a common humanity. For the one Maker fashioned us all; the one Creator breathed life into us all. All of us enjoy the same sky and air, the same days and nights, and though some be good, others bad, some righteous, others unrighteous, God is gracious to all. Christian grace has given great reason for loving our neighbor, for it excludes no one and hence teaches us to look with contempt on no one. No one is to be neglected.

Daily the Lord is grafting shoots of the wild olive from among all nations into the holy branches of his own olive tree. Daily his grace turns enemies into the reconciled, strangers into adopted sons and daughters, and justifies the ungodly.

Leo the Great, "On the Fast of the Tenth Month, I,"
Sermons, sermon 12, sec. 2

Dear Lord, you who came among us to seek and save the lost and to set the captives free, help us to widen our horizons, to make space for the stranger, to watch for those who feel invisible, to give time to the outsider, to talk to the person facing isolation, and to restore justice and value. Give us the courage and determination to join with others in seeing grace in every human face, and the faith to embrace the opportunity in your name. Amen.

FOR REFLECTION: Prov. 24:17; 25:21; Matt. 5:7, 39-41, 43-48; 6:12; 22:37-39; Acts 14:16-17; Rom. 11:11-24; 12:14; Phil. 2:10-11

91

All vices that obstruct our worship of God, all that greed pursues, that pride aspires to, and that luxury lusts for, are destroyed by the virtue of self-restraint. Fasting is meant to aid that virtue. But we must remember fasting is both a spiritual and a physical discipline. It includes far more than not eating certain foods. All sinful desires must be purged. It is a waste of effort to curtail food and not flee from sinful thoughts. A fast that permits us to persist in sinful desires that are more harmful than physical delights is nothing more than an empty bodily exercise. What profit is it to the soul to control the outward person and inwardly be a captive and a slave? What profit is there for the spirit if we issue orders to our limbs but surrender the freedom of our souls?

Therefore, when the body fasts from food, let the spirit fast from vices and pass judgment on all earthly cares and desires according to the law of its King.

LEO THE GREAT, "ON THE FAST OF THE TENTH MONTH, VIII," *SERMONS*, SERMON 19, SEC. 2

O TRIUNE GOD, Father, Son, and Holy Spirit, enlighten me with your saving faith; gladden and strengthen me with your joyful and never-faltering hope; quicken me with your mighty and all-holy love. Subdue and humble me, and guard me with your strongest and most holy fear. Fill me with healing shame from your all-lovely and all-glorious Self for anything found to be contrary to your will. May I not go out from your mercy's presence empty and confounded but as having obtained by grace and faith the gifts of your salvation. All glory be to the Father, to the Son, and to the Holy Spirit. Amen.

ANSELM, ARCHBISHOP OF CANTERBURY, *BOOK OF MEDITATIONS AND PRAYERS*, MEDITATION 8, SEC. 36

FOR REFLECTION: Ps. 19:1-2; 1 Cor. 9:15-18; Gal. 5:16-26; Phil. 4:5; Col. 3:5; 1 Thess. 5:6-8; 1 Tim. 6:11-16

92

Our Savior was born today: let us rejoice! There is no place for sadness when celebrating the birthday of that Life that destroys the fear of death and gives the joy of promised eternity. Let the saint exult because he now draws near to victory. Let the sinner be glad because he is offered pardon. The Son of God, in the fullness of time which the Trinity determined, has assumed our nature to reconcile us to its Author. He did this so that the author of death, the devil, might be conquered through the very nature that Satan had conquered. The Almighty Lord enters the fight, not in the form of his own exalted majesty, but in the form of our humility, our mortality.

The Word of God took on himself our humility without decreasing his own deity. He joined both natures in a union where neither the lower was destroyed in its exaltation nor the higher jeopardized by its humility. Majesty took on humility, strength took on weakness, and eternity took on mortality. To remove our sin, the true God and the true man combined to form one Lord, one Mediator between God and man.

LEO THE GREAT, "ON THE FEAST OF THE NATIVITY, I,"
SERMONS, SERMON 21, SECS. 1-2

O LORD JESUS CHRIST, enable me to gaze on your unspeakable mercy and to tell abroad your goodness toward us. You came down from the bosom of the Father to be born of the Virgin. You suffered on the cross to restore what we had justly lost. Recreate, I beseech you, what once you created, and destroy all that I have done contrary to your will. Destroy in me all that is simply mine, all that you did not create, and recreate all that you have made. Amen.

ANSELM, ARCHBISHOP OF CANTERBURY, *BOOK OF MEDITATIONS AND PRAYERS*,
MEDITATION 6, SEC. 29

FOR REFLECTION: Job 19:4; Luke 1:46-55; 2:1-40; John 1:1-3; Phil. 2:5-11; Heb. 4:14—5:3; 9:11-28

93

In Christ, the loving-kindness of God has been manifest, all the riches of divine goodness showered on us. Our call to eternal life has been assisted by the examples of the Old Testament saints but most importantly in the bodily appearing of the Truth itself. Therefore, we are bound to keep the day of the Lord's nativity without any slothful or carnal delights to obstruct us. This is a day for thoughtfully remembering that by a new birth we are members of the body of Christ and joined to Christ our Head. Let us examine ourselves to make sure we are not ill-fitting members of that body, lest we fail to cohere with the rest of the sacred building.

By the illumination of the Holy Spirit, let us thoughtfully consider who it was who received us into himself and who came to us in the incarnation. While commending the standard of his own gentleness and humility, Christ fills us with the power by which he redeems us. Let us take the yoke of Truth as our governor. Let us imitate our Lord's humility to whose glory we are being conformed: he will lead us to his promises. According to his great mercy he is powerful to forgive and to perfect his gifts in us.

LEO THE GREAT, "ON THE FEAST OF THE NATIVITY, III,"
SERMONS, SERMON 23, SEC. 5

O LORD MY GOD, help me to be obedient without reserve, poor without servility, chaste without compromise, humble without pretense, joyful without depravity, serious without affectation, active without frivolity, submissive without bitterness, truthful without duplicity, fruitful in good works without presumption, quick to revive my neighbor without haughtiness, and quick to edify others by word and example. Amen.

ATTRIBUTED TO THOMAS AQUINAS, "ST. THOMAS OF AQUINAS QUOTES"

✢ ✢ ✢

FOR REFLECTION: Matt. 1:18-25; 11:28-30; Rom. 11:32; 12:11-31; 1 Cor. 6:20; 12:27; 2 Cor. 1:18-22; Eph. 2:4-5; 5:22-33; 1 Tim. 1:12-17

94

As the light of this blessed Christmas morn begins to shed its rays on creation, there floods on our senses the brightness of the wondrous mystery of the incarnation. The birth of our Lord and Savior from the Virgin Mary commends itself to our thoughts as we meditate on divine things. We acknowledge God our Creator. Whether we are engaged in the groans of supplication, shouting praises to God, or offering spiritual sacrifices, no thought should be more frequent than that God the Son of God, though eternally begotten of the coeternal Father, became incarnate through human birth.

On this day, as was so wondrously promised to Mary, the Maker of the world was born of a Virgin's womb. He who created the world became Son of her whom he created. Today the Word of God appeared clothed in flesh, and that which had never been visible to human eyes began to be tangible to our hands. Today the shepherds learned from angels' voices that the Savior was born in the substance of our humanity. Today the essence of the gospel message was announced in the angelic hymn. Now we, too, can sing along with the heavenly host, "Glory in the highest to God, and on earth peace to men of good will."

Leo the Great, "On the Feast of the Nativity, VI,"
Sermons, sermon 26, sec. 1

O God, you make us glad by the yearly festival of the birth of your only Son Jesus Christ: Grant that we, who joyfully receive him as our Redeemer, may with sure confidence behold him when he comes to be our Judge; who lives and reigns with you and the Holy Spirit, one God, now and forever. Amen.

"Nativity of Our Lord: Christmas Day," Collects:
Contemporary, in BCP

FOR REFLECTION: 2 Kings 19:15; Job 12:7-9; 26:7-13; 38:4-38; Pss. 24:1-2; 33:6; 89:11; Luke 1:39-45; 2:8-20; John 1:1-5; 11:32-37

95

The more zealous we become in contending for our salvation, the more determined will be the assaults of the devil and his allies. But always remember that "stronger is he that is in us than he that is against us." Through Christ we become powerful; on his strength we rely.

The Lord permitted himself to be tested so we might be instructed by his example and fortified by his presence. How did Jesus defeat the enemy? In his humanity but not merely by human strength. He drew directly on Scripture and thereby paid great honor to humankind. He inflicted greater defeat on the devil by conquering him in his humanity than by his deity. Jesus overcame Satan just as we can overcome him.

There are no demonstrations of God's power, dearly beloved, apart from trials and temptations. There is no faith without its being tested. There is no contest if there is no foe, no conflict without a battle. If we do not wish to be deceived by snares and spiritual battles, we must be watchful. If we do not want to be overcome, we must fight. Solomon said, "My son, in approaching the service of God prepare your soul for temptation." If we permit the tempter to attack us when we are being careless, he will surely defeat us.

LEO THE GREAT, "ON LENT, I," SERMONS, SERMON 39, SEC. 3

O MY GOD, let all my turning be to you. Give to me the gift of perseverance. Let my soul ever yearn for your glory, my mind love it, my thoughts be intent on it, my whole heart's affection sigh after it, and my tongue speak of it. Let my whole being be held captive by love made perfect. Amen.

ANSELM, ARCHBISHOP OF CANTERBURY, BOOK OF MEDITATIONS AND PRAYERS,
MEDITATION 20, SEC. 102

FOR REFLECTION: Sir. 2:1 (Apocrypha); Matt. 4:1-11; 25:1-13; 26:36-47; Luke 4:1-13; 2 Cor. 1:8-10; Gal. 5:17; Eph. 6:12, 14-17; **1 John 4:4-5**

96

So, dearly beloved, let us who are instructed by the Lord come to spiritual warfare well-informed. The apostle Paul has clearly warned that "our struggle is not against flesh and blood, but against principalities and powers, against the rulers of this dark world, against spiritual wickedness in heavenly things."

The Lord has prepared us well. See with what mighty weapons, with what impregnable defenses, our Commander has armed us. He is renowned for his many victories, the unconquered Master of Christian warfare. He has buckled the belt of truth around our waist, put the breastplate of righteousness in place, and fitted our feet with the gospel of peace. Satan will quickly vanquish an unarmed Christian soldier. In fact, Satan urges us not to be prepared. A Christian who does not have the soldier's footwear will be easily poisoned by the serpent. Christ has given us the shield of faith for the protection of our whole body; on our head he has placed the helmet of salvation; our right hand has been furnished with a sword, that is, with the word of truth. Our Commander has so armed us that not only can we be protected against wounds, but we may also inflict wounds on Satan himself.

LEO THE GREAT, "ON LENT, I," *SERMONS*, SERMON 39, SEC. 4

GLORY TO GOD'S COMPASSION AND MERCY AND LOVE, that he has bestowed such honor and glory on humankind, has made them sons and daughters of the heavenly Father, and called them sisters and brothers of his own. To him be glory forever. Amen.

MACARIUS-SYMEON, *FIFTY SPIRITUAL HOMILIES*, HOMILY 19, SEC. 8

FOR REFLECTION: Ps. 91:1-16; 2 Cor. 10:3-5; **Eph. 6:10-20**; Heb. 2:14; James 4:7; 1 Pet. 5:8; 1 John 5:4-5

97

Freely taking the form of a servant, our Lord, in whom alone was humankind's nature resident without fault, obediently championed our cause.

Carrying torches and lanterns, the sons of darkness assailed the true Light in Gethsemane. But torches and lanterns could not provide escape from the darkness of unbelief. So they could not recognize the Fountain of light. They arrested Jesus, not because they had power over him, but because he was willing to be seized and led away. Had he not been willing, wicked men could have done him no harm. However, had he not been willing, our salvation would have slipped away.

O inexpressible glory of the Lord's passion. In the cross are contained the Lord's sovereign plans, the world's judgment, and the power of the Crucified! The cross is the fount of all blessings and source of all graces. Through it believers receive strength for their weaknesses, glory in exchange for their shame, and life instead of death. By the one offering of Christ's body and blood he has become the true "Lamb of God, who takes away the sins of the world."

LEO THE GREAT, "ON THE PASSION, VIII: ON WEDNESDAY IN HOLY WEEK," *SERMONS*, SERMON 59, SECS. 1, 7

O LORD, you did not refuse to be crowned with thorns, yet you save us from the wounds of sin. In your thirst you accepted the bitterness of gall, yet you fill us with eternal delights. You tasted death, yet you give eternal life to the dead. To you, O Lord, with the Father and the Spirit, be glory, majesty, dominion, and authority. Amen.

FROM A PRAYER BY GREGORY THE GREAT, "PRAYER OF ACCLAIM TO THE SUFFERING CHRIST," SAINTS.SQPN.COM

FOR REFLECTION: Isa. 65:2; Matt. 12:22-32; **John 1:29-33**; 10:1-21; 17:1-5; 18:1-8; Eph. 5:1-2; Heb. 10:1-10, 14, 18

GREGORY THE GREAT

How does a person gain the enduring appellation "the Great"? In the case of Pope Gregory the Great (ca. AD 540–604) it was because of the outstanding quality of his authentic servant leadership in times that called for just such a person. The excellence he inherited from his family was unreservedly given to Christ and his church.

Gregory was born in Rome of a senatorial family. When about age thirty-three, Emperor Justin II (ca. AD 520-78) appointed him governor of Rome. But the monastic life was far more appealing. Instead of grasping to preserve what he had inherited, a year later Gregory devoted all his wealth to feed the poor and to establish monasteries. Then he entered the monastery of St. Andrew. But Gregory discovered that he was too much an activist to be a good monk, even though his interest in extending and regulating monastic life continued.

In AD 579 Pope Pelagius II (pope from 579 to 590) dispatched Gregory as ambassador to the court of Constantinople. About seven years later, he returned to Rome as the abbot of St. Andrew. In AD 590 Gregory the monk was chosen pope, the first monk to serve in that capacity.

As pope, Gregory contributed in many ways that led to his greatness. Reading his extensive pastoral counsel will elicit increasing esteem for him and his work. While Gregory is not remembered for theological originality, he is certainly known for his faithfulness to the apostolic faith. He presented Augustine to the Middle Ages. Beyond that, his bold visionary administration of the church, at a time when the influence of the papacy had declined, was among the greatest in the church's history. In addition to the demands placed on him as spiritual head of the church, Gregory had to raise an army to ward off a threatened invasion of Rome by the Lombards. He efficiently managed lands owned by the church, not to swell the church's coffers, but to support the work of ministry and public worship and to provide for various charitable foundations.

As a missionary pope, Gregory was strategically instrumental in the conversion of England, as well as in turning many Arian Lombards to the orthodox faith. He is also remembered as a great preacher, for developing the Gregorian chants, and for his writings that were popular throughout the Middle Ages.

98

("[Job] was blameless and upright; he feared God and shunned evil"
[Job 1:1, NIV].)

Undoubtedly, whoever longs for the eternal country will live sincerely and righteously. He will be holy in practice and sound in faith, sincere in the good that he does in the body, and pure in the inner person. Some people are not pure in the good deeds they perform. Instead, they seek not the reward that enriches the spirit but favor and rewards from others. Hence it is well said by a certain wise man, "Woe to the sinner who follows two ways," meaning when a good deed supposedly belongs to God but in fact belongs to self-glory and the sinful world.

Job "feared God and eschewed evil." Out of fear the church of Christ starts on the path toward humility and righteousness. But it advances and completes the journey in love.

When Job is said to have "feared God," it is correctly noted that he also "eschewed evil." Fear comes first. Love follows. When this happens, the fear that has been left behind is trampled under foot by holy desires of the heart.

GREGORY THE GREAT, MORALS ON THE BOOK OF JOB,
VOL. I, PT. I, BK. I, SECS. I-2, 34, 36-37

O LORD, teach my heart where and how to seek you. I come as a beggar to the Rich, a sinner to the All-Merciful. Let me enter the closet of your heart. By your Spirit, who enables us to cry, "Abba, Father," assist me to say, "I seek your face; your face, O Lord, will I seek." Amen.

ANSELM, ARCHBISHOP OF CANTERBURY, BOOK OF MEDITATIONS AND PRAYERS,
MEDITATION 21, SEC. 103

FOR REFLECTION: Job 1:1-3; Ps. 37:27; Eccles. 1:18; 2:12; Song of Sol. 2:2; **Sir. 2:12** (Apocrypha); Jer. 2:5-12, 20-22, 26-30; Matt. 10:16; **Rom. 8:15**; 16:19; 1 Cor. 14:20; Phil. 2:15; James 1:22-25; 2 Pet. 2:7-8; Rev. 2:13

99

Christian virtues are destitute if they stand alone. Wisdom, for example, is less valuable if it lacks comprehension. But comprehension is useless unless it rests on wisdom. Even if comprehension can unlock great mysteries, unless it is joined to wisdom, it just sets itself for a fall. And counsel is worthless when fortitude is lacking. What counsel can discern by turning things over and over will never be executed if fortitude is missing. But fortitude breaks down unless it is supported by counsel. This is because the greater the power fortitude says it possesses, the more miserably it rushes headlong into ruin without the governance of reason. Take knowledge as another illustration. Knowledge is nothing unless it serves holiness, for if it is not harnessed to the practice of the good, it brings itself more severely under judgment. Piety is useless if it lacks discernment, for when piety lacks the enlightenment of knowledge, it doesn't know how to show mercy. Unless piety is joined to the other virtues, fear will rise up and render it paralyzed.

One virtue is refreshed by another. They feast in the company of each other, as if each one were supposed to prepare a banquet for the others. When the virtues invite faith, hope, and love to the feasts, there will be rejoicing over all the virtues.

GREGORY THE GREAT, *MORALS ON THE BOOK OF JOB*,
VOL. I, PT. I, BK. I, SECS. 45-46

I HOPE IN YOU, O my God. I humbly trust that you will pardon my sins for the sake of your dear Son Jesus Christ. Cleanse my sinful soul in his precious blood and make me holy and bring me safe to everlasting life. Amen.
"ACTS OF FAITH, HOPE, AND LOVE," A SHORT SERVICE OF COMFORT AND HOPE FOR SICK COMMUNICANTS, IN A BOOK OF OFFICES (1914)

FOR REFLECTION: Matt. 5:6; 6:33; Luke 18:9-14; John 14:6; 17:7; 2 Cor. 8:21; Gal. 5:22-23; Eph. 4:14-15; Phil. 2:3-11; 1 Thess. 5:6-8

100

The Scriptures have been set before us as a mirror to reveal our inner selves. We learn both the beauties and the deformities that mark us. Scriptures alert us to progress we have made as Christ's disciples and teach us how to advance. The Scriptures tell of the deeds of the saints and stir the hearts of the weak to follow them. When the Bible celebrates the victories of the saints, it gives us strength to confront our own temptations. The struggles and victories of God's people encourage us not to be dismayed by the conflicts we encounter. The Bible presents not only the excellencies of the saints but also their trials and even failures. In their victories we see examples we should follow and good reason for hope; in their failures we see the importance of cautious humility and what should be feared and avoided.

Look therein and see how Job was made stronger by overcoming temptation but how David was brought low because he yielded to temptation. Let us be lifted to joy by the former and kept humble by the latter. We will never be crippled by fear and despair if we receive hope and confidence from the victories of God's people.

GREGORY THE GREAT, *Morals on the Book of Job*,
VOL. I, PT. I, BK. 2, SEC. I

O GREAT SHEPHERD OF THE CHURCH, may we all be guarded by you, as from feeding in a poisoned and deadly pasture. Guide us away from it, that we may be one in Christ Jesus our Lord, now and until we feed in the heavenly pasture. To whom be the glory and the might forever and ever. Amen.

FOR REFLECTION: Luke 24:13-27; Acts 2:14-36; 8:26-35; 13:13-51; 1 Pet. 1:8

101

There are two types of troublesome and objectionable speech. The first type commends what is erroneous and deficient. The second type is always looking for some way to complain about what is good and upright. The first type is hurled along by the current. The second type places itself close to the channels of truth to block it. Fear of the truth dominates the first type; arrogance elevates the other. By offering applause, the first type tries to win favor. Contentious anger drives the second type. On command, the first type is willing to grovel; opposition inflates and propels the second type.

They who give themselves to mischievous speech plunder the estate of righteousness. The mind may be compared to an elevated lake of water. Its resources can be wasted by many pointless streams flowing from it. Superfluous words that escape the confines of silence are like the many streams that dissipate the lake.

What then should we do? The tongue must be wisely kept under strict control. But this doesn't mean it should be chained for fear that when turned loose it will always cause mischief. Instead, it must be trained always to render service to the Lord.

GREGORY THE GREAT, *MORALS ON THE BOOK OF JOB*,
VOL. 1, PT. 2, BK. 7, SECS. 57-61

O LORD, the lodging of my soul is too narrow; enlarge it so that you can enter it. It is ruinous; repair it. It contains that which offends your eyes; cleanse it. I confess and know this to be true. To whom should I cry, save you? Lord, cleanse me from my secret faults, and spare your servant from the power of the enemy. Amen.

AUGUSTINE, BISHOP OF HIPPO, *CONFESSIONS*, BK. 1, CHAP. 5, SEC. 6

FOR REFLECTION: Pss. 19:14; 140:11; 141:3; Prov. 12:18; 15:3; 17:14; 18:4, 21; 26:10; Matt. 12:33-37; 15:18; Eph. 4:29; Col. 3:5-11; James 1:19, 26; 3:1-12

102

Christ our Head has called us to be his members, that through the bond of love and faith he might make us one body in himself. Therefore it is only reasonable that we obey him with all our hearts. Unless he is working in us, we can do nothing to obey his will. But through him we can obey his call. Therefore, let nothing divide us from the citadel of our Head, for if we deny the bond of love and faith to our brothers and sisters, we will also be separated from Christ. We will wither like branches cast off from the vine. Therefore, so that we may be counted worthy to be the dwelling place of our Redeemer, let us abide in his love with unadulterated sincerity. Jesus told us, "He that loves me will keep my word, and my Father will love him, and we will come to him and make our abode with him."

We cannot stay close to the Author of our salvation unless we cut away from our lives all covetousness, the root of all evil. In obedience to the Lord's commands, let us banish from the temple of Christ all avarice, which amounts to worshiping idols in the church of Christ. We must permit nothing to enter the temple of Christ that will harm it and nothing that is disorderly.

GREGORY THE GREAT, *Epistles*, BK. 9, EPISTLE 106

O LORD OUR GOD, whose might is incomparable, whose glory is incomprehensible, whose mercy is immeasurable, and whose love for us is ineffable: from the tenderness of your heart look down upon us, for to you belong all glory, honor, and worship, Father, Son, and Holy Spirit, now and forever, and to the ages of ages. Amen.

JOHN CHRYSOSTOM, IN *The Divine Liturgy of St. John Chrysostomos*, THE ORTHODOX CHRISTIAN PAGE

FOR REFLECTION: Prov. 3:9; 21:27; Mic. 2:1-2; Matt. 6:19-21; 16:24-27; 18:20; **John 14:23-31**; Rom. 12:9-21; Eph. 4:20–5:14

103

(Gregory the Great persistently condemned simony, the scandalous practice of buying and selling ecclesiastical offices. The following paraphrase applies to all impure service in the body of Christ.)

When our Lord and Redeemer cleansed the temple, he overthrew the seats of those who sold doves. What else is it to sell doves in the temple but to seek an office in the church for selfish and sordid reasons? Such a practice amounts to trying to buy and sell the Holy Spirit. We should be filled with sorrowful disgust when foul gain has any place in the church. It reveals the contagion of sin.

Whoever selfishly seeks office or position in the church does so out of avarice, not because he loves the body of Christ. He is fixated on the benefits of the position, not on glorifying our Lord. When a person seizes position in the church, he proves himself all the more unworthy. What does such a person accomplish in trying to climb higher but to fall lower? He rises outwardly but sinks inwardly. Therefore, let pure hearts prevail. Let service in Christ's body not result from salesmanship but from the wisdom and calling of God.

GREGORY THE GREAT, *EPISTLES*, BK. 9, EPISTLE 106

THOU IMAGE OF THE INVISIBLE GOD, the Firstborn over all creation, in your Father and by the Spirit you have rescued us from the dominion of darkness and brought us into the kingdom of God. Set our hearts on things above, and fill us with all spiritual wisdom and understanding. For to you belongs all glory, honor, and worship, to the Father and to the Holy Spirit, now and forever. Amen.

FOR REFLECTION: Deut. 18:20-22; Ps. 69:9; Prov. 21:27; Jer. 23:30-32; Matt. 10:8; 21:33-46; John 2:12-17; 8:44; Acts 8:9-25; 1 Tim. 3:8-13

104

When Satan fails to invade the Christian soul by using openly sinful devices, he next tempts Christians to practice a superficial show of piety. For example, he will try to persuade them to receive ill-gotten money and then give it to the poor as righteous alms. What the devil wants to do in this instance is inject his poison and disguise it as almsgiving. The fowler would not capture the bird of prey if traps were in plain sight, and the fisherman would not catch fish if hooks were not hidden by bait.

By all means, the cunning of Satan is to be feared and guarded against, lest those he cannot subvert by open temptation, he should succeed in slaying with his hidden weapons. Giving of what has been obtained illicitly must not be counted as righteous almsgiving.

Gifts that please our Redeemer are those that come as pure gifts from the Lord. Let us never gain anything through sin and pretense. The Holy Scriptures have warned that "the sacrifices of the impious are abominable," especially when brought with evil intent.

GREGORY THE GREAT, *EPISTLES*, BK. 9, EPISTLE 106

O ALMIGHTY GOD, seeing that in all things pertaining to Satan's crafty devices there is need for the help of divine grace, we implore your protection and guidance with continual prayers in order to live righteously. Without your enabling presence we cannot hope to rise to live righteously in Christ Jesus. Amen.

BASED ON GREGORY THE GREAT, *EPISTLES*, BK. 9, EPISTLE 106

FOR REFLECTION: Prov. 3:9; **21:27**; **15:8**; Sir. 34:24 (Apocrypha); Matt. 4:1-11; 13:3-9; 22:15-21; Mark 14:1-2; Luke 4:1-15; John 8:44; Acts 5:1-11; James 4:7; 1 Pet. 5:8-11

105

We must vigilantly guard against the snares of the devil, our ancient foe. The greater the gifts of God he sees among us, the more subtle are his snares for stealing them. Robbers don't wait on the road for travelers who carry nothing of value. They wait for travelers carrying gold and silver. Our life on earth is a road. Christians must be on guard against being ambushed and having their gifts stolen. We must protect God's gifts through humility and in purity. "Everyone that exalts himself shall be humbled, and he that humbles himself shall be exalted." The person who loves what is heavenly will not cut himself or herself off from the root of humility.

Often that malignant spirit, the devil, will agitate a Christian worker with thoughts of self-glory. If the devil succeeds, then a deadly tumor will grow and deprive the Christian of the grace of the Lord who gave the gifts. Then will be applied the words of the prophet, "Having trust in your beauty, you played the harlot because of your renown." When Satan tries to use the good things we have done to exalt us in pride, let us confess our sin and remember it is only the grace of Almighty God, not our own abilities, that keeps us from falling.

GREGORY THE GREAT, *Epistles*, BK. 9, EPISTLE 122

AND NOW, O MOST GRACIOUS GOD, Father and Fountain of mercy and goodness, fill us with such a keen sensitivity to and persuasion regarding all the great truths revealed to us in the gospel of Jesus Christ. May they influence and govern our lives, and through the Holy Spirit, may the lives that we lead fully proceed from faith in the Son of God. Amen.

HENRY SCOUGAL, *The Life of God in the Soul of Man*, PT. 3

FOR REFLECTION: Ezek. 16:15-19; Luke 14:7-11; 18:14; 1 Cor. 3:17; 2 Cor. 8:7; Gal. 6:1-9; Phil. 3:1-21; 1 Thess. 4:3; 1 Pet. 1:1-17

106

(The following letter is a sterling example of Christian humility and unity. Gregory writes to John, abbot of Mount Siena, head of a hospital for the elderly that was suffering a critical shortage of beds and bedding.)

The humility of your epistle testifies to the holiness of your life. Thanks be to Almighty God, for there are persons like you who pray for us. We labor under the responsibilities of church government; we are tossed to and fro in the billows that often overwhelm us. But by the protecting hand of God's grace we are raised from the deep. May you, who by contrast lead a tranquil life and stand, as it were, safe on the shore, extend to us your hand of prayer. May your intercessions help us reach the land of the living. Pray not only for your own life but also for our rescue. May God safeguard your love with the right hand of his protection. Through prayer, wisdom, admonition and a godly example, feed the flock charged to your care. May you and your flock reach the pastures of eternal life. We will explore the heavenly pastures in all their beauty when we reach the green pastures of eternal life.

GREGORY THE GREAT, *EPISTLES*, BK. 11, EPISTLE 1

> *WHILE LIFE SHALL LAST, my thankful lips*
> *A song to God will raise,*
> *And while my being I possess,*
> *My Maker I will praise.*
> *My heart shall think upon his grace*
> *In meditation sweet;*
> *My soul, rejoicing in the Lord,*
> *His praises shall repeat. Amen.*

THE PSALTER: WITH RESPONSIVE READINGS (1912), NO. 288, HYMNARY

FOR REFLECTION: Ps. 10:17-18; Prov. 29:23; Isa. 57:15; Luke 12:32; 18:10-14; John 10:27; Acts 20:18-38; 1 Pet. 5:1-11

107

(In a letter to Paschasius, bishop of Naples, Gregory reprimands Christians who have tried to force Jews to become Christians. His counsel reaches farther than the Jews.)

When we seek to win someone to Christ, we should be students of kindness, not students of bitterness and acrimony. Otherwise, those who might have been won to Christ through kindness will be driven away by our harshness and denunciation. Desiring to convert others, some people want to force non-Christians to abandon their own religion and way of life.

Take the Jews, for example. In an effort to win Jews to Christ, some Christians condemn the Jewish holy days, their feasts and way of life. Christians who treat Jews this way are creating trouble that will lead to no good. Why should we treat the Jews in ways that succeed only in driving them away from Christ? They should be free to observe and celebrate all their festivals and holidays.

When dealing with Jews or anyone else, we must appeal to them with reason and treat them kindly. We must behave toward people in ways that might make them want to follow Christ rather than flee from him.

GREGORY THE GREAT, *EPISTLES*, BK. 13, EPISTLE 12

O THOU SHEPHERD AND RULER OF ALL, by the Holy Spirit place a word of comfort, edification, and exhortation in my mouth. Encourage the good to aspire to better things, and recall to the path of righteousness those who have gone astray. Above all, may you give the Spirit of wisdom and revelation to express your saving love to all. Amen.

ANSELM, ARCHBISHOP OF CANTERBURY, *BOOK OF MEDITATIONS AND PRAYERS*, MEDITATION 18, SEC. 90

FOR REFLECTION: Matt. 10:7-14; Luke 6:27-36; 15:1-32; 19:1-10; Rom. 1:1-6; 9:1-5; 10:1-4; 17:36; 1 Cor. 9:2; 13:4-7; Col. 3:12-17; 4:2-6

ANSELM, ARCHBISHOP OF CANTERBURY

Anselm (ca. AD 1033–1109), archbishop of Canterbury, left a major footprint on Christian doctrine and philosophy. He believed rigorous theological and philosophical thought are essential for maintaining the integrity of Christian doctrine. But transforming faith must come first. Through careful reflection, faith seeks to understand God and his ways.

Anselm, a doctor of the church, was born in Italy and was educated in Normandy. He became a Benedictine monk, a teacher, and the abbot (head) of the monastery of Bec in Normandy. In 1094 he became the second archbishop of Canterbury, England.

Anselm's writings and explanations of the faith have found their way into informed discussions of Christian doctrine. His shorter works include *On Free Will* and *The Fall of the Devil*, in which he explains why Satan rebelled. In the lengthier work *Why the God-Man?* Anselm answers the question, "Why did the Son of God become incarnate and then suffer and die on the cross?" Only the incarnate sinless Son of God could make restitution, compensation, or satisfaction for humankind's sin against the Holy God and the demands of the law. Because Christ made the restitution humanity owed, God can now justly set aside punishment. Christ opened the door of reconciliation.

Anselm's process of argumentation set the stage for scholasticism, a form of thought that characterized most of the Middle Ages. He is also important for the ways he attempted to prove God's existence, the most famous of which is the ontological argument in the *Proslogion*. The "fool" described in the Psalms (14:1) was a fool because he thought that by denying some finitely existing thing, a "god" small enough to deny, he had successfully denied God's existence. In fact, God is that Being than which no greater being can be conceived, an *infinite* Being for which a *finite* mind cannot account. If anyone thinks he or she has successfully denied God, he or she has not thought high enough. Only God can account for the idea or knowledge of such a God present in the mind.

Anselm's *Meditations and Prayers* are a treasury of nurture in Christian discipleship.

108

Awake, my soul, awake. Let the fire of love from heaven blaze in your inmost parts. Consider the dignity the Lord God has bestowed on you. And learning, revere him with the language of a holy life. He who has given you a dwelling in himself, who desires to make of you a temple for his dwelling, does he not adorn you with himself? To be baptized in Christ is to be clothed by Christ. What praise will you then give him who has invested you with such grace and exalted you with such dignity? Let my soul's greatest outburst of joy be to exclaim that God has clothed me with the garments of his salvation. The angels' supreme joy is to gaze on the Son of God. But this is the One who in mercy condescended to clothe us with himself.

These are the glorious benefits of our Creator. If we ponder them correctly, embrace them devoutly, and imitate them with a fervent love, not only will we recover the good things lost through Adam, but through our Savior's inexhaustible grace there will be much higher possessions. For God himself, in Christ, has been made our elder Brother through the mystery of the incarnation. Therefore, apply yourself without weariness to the pursuit of holiness.

ANSELM, ARCHBISHOP OF CANTERBURY, *BOOK OF MEDITATIONS AND PRAYERS*, MEDITATION 1, SECS. 1-6

O LORD, enable me to consider all your benefits. Remove all delights that might be opposed to you. Let no solace of the present allure me from you. Embrace me with your love and fill me with holy longing. To you be unending praise. Amen.
ANSELM, ARCHBISHOP OF CANTERBURY, *BOOK OF MEDITATIONS AND PRAYERS*, MEDITATION 1, SEC. 6

FOR REFLECTION: Gen. 1:26; Exod. 3:14; Song of Sol. 1:1, 3; Sir. 47:10 (Apocrypha); Isa. 61:10; Luke 17:21; John 12:32; 14:4; 15:4; 17:21; 27:21; Acts 17:28; 1 Cor. 1:30; 3:17; 11:7; 2 Cor. 6:16; Gal. 3:27; Eph. 5:32

109

(Why the God-man? Why the incarnation?)

Dear Christian, raised from sin's death, redeemed from miserable slavery, and set free by the blood of God incarnate, consider the meaning of your redemption. Reflect on the Source of your salvation. Taste the goodness of your Redeemer. Break forth in fires of love for your Savior. Savor the honeycomb of your being crucified and risen with Christ; swallow its health.

Christ, the Good Samaritan, has healed you. He, the good Friend, has redeemed you with his life and set you free. So the virtue of your salvation is Christ's virtue. But where does his virtue reside? You know his hands were angrily fastened to the arms of the cross. But O what strength there is in that apparent weakness. What grandeur in his humility! What holiness in the contempt he bore!

O hidden strength, that God incarnate, bound to a tree, should liberate those fast bound by perpetual death. O veiled omnipotence, that God incarnate, condemned to die with thieves, should release those vandalized by demons. O divine virtue concealed, that God incarnate given over to torture should extricate innumerable souls from hell.

ANSELM, ARCHBISHOP OF CANTERBURY, *BOOK OF MEDITATIONS AND PRAYERS*,
MEDITATION 11, SEC. 51

BLESSED LORD, by the Holy Spirit enable us to follow you in obedience to the Father. Not by necessity did you take upon yourself the cross of shame but of your own free election. May I render you the homage of a thankful love for your merciful free choice on my behalf. Amen.

ANSELM, ARCHBISHOP OF CANTERBURY, *BOOK OF MEDITATIONS AND PRAYERS*,
MEDITATION 11, SECS. 51-52

FOR REFLECTION: Isa. 53:1-12; Hab. 3:4; Mark 4:35-41; Luke 1:26-33, 46-55; 2:1-22; John 1:1-18; Acts 2:14-39; Rom. 1:18-31; 1 Cor. 1:15-23; Eph. 1:3-14

110

Contemplation of our Savior's most holy birth is brimful of joy, of mercy, and of edification: of joy because of our own exceeding gladness, of mercy because of our Lord's sufferings, and of edification because of the lessons the incarnation teaches us. For what is more joyful than to behold as incarnate the One who, as we know, is humankind's Creator? What, again, should seem to us more astonishing than to see with unveiled eyes that in the person of this Mediator between God and man, our Lord Jesus Christ, after a certain wondrous and incomprehensible manner, eternity began to dwell among us? In him majesty is shrouded in humility. Though eternal in the bosom of the Father, he was conceived in a mother's womb. Of the Father from eternity without beginning, he is born in time of his mother without a human father. Behold! He who clothed the earth with trees and vegetation, who strung the sky with lights, who peopled the earth and stocked the seas, here lies wrapped in rags. He whom the heaven of heavens cannot contain is confined in a narrow manger and is fed with a mother's milk. All praise be to God, the Father of our Lord Jesus Christ, who has so richly and marvelously blessed us in Christ.

ANSELM, ARCHBISHOP OF CANTERBURY, *BOOK OF MEDITATIONS AND PRAYERS*, MEDITATION 12, SEC. 55

O GOD of unchangeable power and eternal light, let the whole world see and know that all things are being brought to their perfection by him through whom all things were made, your Son Jesus Christ our Lord, who lives and reigns with you, in the unity of the Holy Spirit, one God, forever and ever. Amen.

"THE PRESENTATION," THE ORDINATION OF A DEACON, IN BCP

FOR REFLECTION: Matt. 1:18-25; Luke 2:1-7; John 1:1-5; Eph. 3:9; Col. 1:16; 1 Tim. 2:1-5; Heb. 1:1-4; 8:16; 9:15; 12:18-24; 1 Pet. 1:17-21; 1 John 1:1-4; Rev. 1:12-20; 3:14

111

(The Lord Jesus Christ is the Wisdom and Power of God.)

O wondrous scene! In Jesus Christ eternity begins to *be*. He is the Wisdom, whose wisdom has neither beginning nor end. Yet he, the very Wisdom of God, *advances* from less to greater. He whose eternity cannot be decreased, even as it cannot be increased, lives among us, his time among us *measured* in days and hours. The primal Author of grace, its Preserver and its Giver, *grows* in grace. He whom all creation adores, and to whom every knee shall bow, is *made subject* to human parents. He whom angels serve is *tempted* by the devil.

Behold and stand amazed! The Bread of Life hungers; the Fountain thirsts; the Way grows weary; Greatness is subjected to the malice of others; Might is weakened; Power wearies; Divine Glory is despised and mocked; Joy mourns; Gladness weeps at the death of a friend; Majesty is shrouded in humility, and Life in death.

ANSELM, ARCHBISHOP OF CANTERBURY, BOOK OF MEDITATIONS AND PRAYERS, MEDITATION 12, SEC. 55

WHEN, O GOD, I consider all your wonderful works, I tremble with amazement, for you shine forth all glorious in all of them. Yet, great though the creation is, and beautiful and very good, it stands empty of beauty when compared with you. Earth and sky and all their grandeur subsist by you, their Creator and Governor. They speak forth your power and fullness, your wisdom and beauty, your goodness and love. As the light excels darkness, so you transcend them all. "What besides you can I desire more on this earth?" Amen.

ANSELM, ARCHBISHOP OF CANTERBURY, BOOK OF MEDITATIONS AND PRAYERS, MEDITATION 13, SEC. 62

FOR REFLECTION: Ps. 73:25; Matt. 4:1-11; Luke 2:41-52; 13:31-35; 22:63-65; John 4:1-38; 11:17-44; 19:1-30; Acts 2:22-36; Rom. 11:33-36; 14:9-12; Phil. 2:5-11; Heb. 2:5-18

BERNARD OF CLAIRVAUX

The remarkable record of service to Christ and his church left by Bernard of Clairvaux (AD 1090–1153) marks him as a giant of Christian discipleship and teaching. He was a major leader of the church in the first half of the twelfth century and remains a towering guide for Christian spirituality. Yet there is nothing in his record to indicate Bernard ever saw himself as anything other than a thoroughly graced servant of the Lord.

He was born in Fontaine-lès-Dijon to parents of the highest nobility who carefully oversaw his education. At age nine he was sent to a famous school, where he excelled in the study of poetry and literature, an interest motivated by his love for Scripture. He would later become a poet of the sufferings of Jesus, and the virginity of Mary.

In 1112 Bernard entered the Abbey of Citeaux, where he received an education in monastic formation. In 1115 he was sent to establish a new monastery in Clairvaux, or the Valley of Light. As a young abbot, Bernard published sermons on Gabriel's announcement to Mary. Those sermons marked him as a gifted writer and teacher. His fame and personal charm drew many to Clairvaux. He would later invest his abilities in a reform of Cistercian monasteries.

News of Bernard's talents spread far beyond monastic circles. Rulers sought his counsel. His most famous service as a counselor came in 1130 when he helped heal a dispute that had bred division in the papacy and the church. Bernard also worked to bring peace between France and England. At the request of a former student, Pope Eugene III, in 1145 Bernard preached the beginning of the Second Crusade. In the closing years of his life, Bernard rose from his sickbed and traveled to Rhineland to defend Jews against persecution.

In addition to his astonishing productivity in establishing Cistercian monasteries, Bernard wrote many works of Christian formation that teach growth in Christian holiness. For example, his *On Loving God* maps the path by which God's grace guides Christians to perfect love for God.

Bernard died at Clairvaux in 1153.

112

Why should we love God, and in what measure? The reason for loving God is God himself. And the extent to which God should be loved is immeasurable.

Could any greater claim be made on our love than that Christ freely gave himself for unworthy sinners? What more regal gift could God have offered?

Ought not God to be loved in return when we consider *who* loved, *whom* he loved, and *how much* he loved? For *who* is he that loved us? The One Christians confess, "You are my God." Is this not the ultimate demonstration of that love that refuses to seek its own interests?

For *whom* was such inexpressible love demonstrated? To God's enemies, for "when we were enemies, we were reconciled to God by the death of his Son." So it was God Almighty who loved us freely and loved us while we were still his enemies.

And *how* great is God's love? He "so loved the world that he gave his only begotten Son." And what about the *measure* of God's love? "He did not spare his own Son but delivered him up for us all." This is the claim that the holy, supreme, and omnipotent God has on us who were defiled. God has wondrously offered his love so that we need no longer remain in our sins.

BERNARD OF CLAIRVAUX, *ON LOVING GOD*, CHAP. I

O LORD MY GOD, also bestow on me understanding to know you, zeal to seek you, wisdom to find you, a life that is pleasing to you, unshakable perseverance, and a hope that will one day be fulfilled in your glorious presence. Amen.

ATTRIBUTED TO THOMAS AQUINAS, "PRAYERS BY ST. THOMAS AQUINAS," 2 HEARTS NETWORK

FOR REFLECTION: Pss. 16:2; 63:1-8; 73:23-26; **John 3:16-18**; 15:9-17; 17:20-23; **Rom. 5:10-11**; **8:31-39**; 1 Cor. 13:5; Col. 1:21-23; 1 John 4:7-21

113

No benefit is derived from having a gift if one does not know he possesses it. But some people who know they possess a gift fail to recognize it came from God. Instead, they glorify themselves, believing the gift resulted from their own efforts. They commit the sin of vainglory by failing to glorify God as the Giver of all good things. The apostle Paul asked, "What have you that you did not receive?" If all that we have is a gift from God, then why engage in self-glory and act as though it were not given? Proper glory glorifies God in all things, for the Lord alone is the Truth. Recognize the value of the gift, but don't glory over it as your own.

As God's people we must know *first* what we *are* and *second* that we *are not* of ourselves. Unless Jesus' disciples thoroughly understand this truth, they will fail to glorify God, and their glorying will be in vain. If Jesus' disciples do not with thanksgiving rejoice over God's gifts of grace, they will end up living as beasts that perish.

BERNARD OF CLAIRVAUX, *ON LOVING GOD*, CHAP. 2

NOW LET MY PRAISE and blessing and thanksgiving be rendered to you, O Lord my God, for all your gifts and bounties, no merits of mine requiring, nay, my sins notwithstanding. You have lavished benefits on me in soul and body. Such have been your mercies and goodness that I now see that you have blessed me from my cradle. But I pray you, Lord, I pray you, let me never be unthankful for such great benefits or forgetful of so many mercies. Amen.

ANSELM, ARCHBISHOP OF CANTERBURY, *BOOK OF MEDITATIONS AND PRAYERS*, MEDITATION 18, SEC. 91

FOR REFLECTION: Pss. 35:18; 50:14; 75:1; Song of Sol. 1:8; John 14:6; **1 Cor.** 1:31; **4:7**; Rom. 8:31-32; Eph. 5:15-20; Heb. 12:13-16; Rev. 11:17

114

If a person is ignorant of the fact that he is distinguished from the lower creatures for no reason other than God's special gifts, he will soon betray his God-given dignity and begin to behave like some of the creatures. His ignorance will result in bondage to passions, and he will increasingly resemble creatures not made in God's image.

Christians must be vigilant. We must neither rank ourselves too low in God's order of creation nor think of ourselves too highly. The latter error follows from foolishly crediting to our own accomplishments what good might be found in us. But there is a kindred and more grievous error: the sin of presumption, which means intentionally and arrogantly usurping God's glory for oneself because of goods that are God's alone. While ignorance may be brutish, arrogance is satanic.

To guard against the sin of presumption, virtue must be added to dignity and wisdom. Virtue will seek and find the Author and Giver of all that is good.

BERNARD OF CLAIRVAUX, *On Loving God*, CHAP. 2

AUTHOR AND FOUNTAIN OF ALL LIFE AND BLESSEDNESS! We rejoice to consider what beautiful things you will accomplish in those who yield themselves to you. O that the holy life of the blessed Jesus, and the excellent graces that appeared so eminently in him, would always be the pattern for our formation. May we never cease our pursuit of our Lord's likeness till that new and divine nature reigns in us. For to you belong all glory, honor, and worship, to the Father, Son, and Holy Spirit, now and ever, and unto the ages of ages. Amen.

HENRY SCOUGAL, *The Life of God in the Soul of Man*, PT. I

FOR REFLECTION: Gen. 1:26-27; 8:21; Exod. 20:4; 23:24; Lev. 26:1; Deut. 5:8; Pss. 94:10; 136:25; Luke 12:47; Rom. 1:18-32; 8:29; 1 Cor. 15:49; 2 Cor. 3:18; 4:4; Col. 3:10

115

(Of Love and Its Recompense)

Love is an affection of the soul, not a contract. It is neither given nor received on the basis of a mere agreement. Instead, love is spontaneous in its origin. If you love to gain something else in return, then what you really love is that "something else." Paul did not preach the gospel because he wanted to earn bread. No, he ate so that he might be strengthened to preach the gospel. What he loved was not bread but the gospel.

On a lower level, it is the reluctant, not the eager, whom we urge by promising rewards. Who would think of paying a person to do what he already longs to do? No one would hire a hungry person to eat, a thirsty person to drink, or a mother to nurse her infant. Who would think of bribing a farmer to dress his own vineyard, cultivate his orchard, or repair his dwelling? So all the more, one who loves God truly asks no other recompense than God himself. If he should require anything more, it would be the prize he loves, not God himself.

Bernard of Clairvaux, *On Loving God*, chap. 7

I love you, O my God, above all things, because you have been so good, so patient, so loving to me, notwithstanding all the sins by which I have so grievously offended you. I love you, O blessed Jesus, my Savior, because you did suffer so much for love of me, an ungrateful sinner, and did die on the cross for my salvation.

O make me love you more and more, and show my love to you by faithfully keeping your commandments all the days of my life. Amen.

"Acts of Faith, Hope, and Love," A Short Service of Comfort and Hope for Sick Communicants, in A Book of Offices (1914)

FOR REFLECTION: Pss. 18:1-3; 63:1-3, 7-8; 84:2-4; Matt. 26:36-46; Mark 10:17-27; Luke 14:27-28; John 14:20-23; 1 Cor. 13:5; Phil. 1:9-11; 1 Pet. 1:7-9

116

At first a person may "love" God because of the benefits he derives, not because of who God is. But can such a person not see how little he can do by himself and how radically dependent he is on God's goodness? Such recognition should cause a person to abandon his self-centered disposition toward God. When recurring tribulations cause a person to flee to God for his unfailing help, would not even a heart as hard as iron and as cold as marble be softened by the Savior's goodness? Would not a person turn away from loving God selfishly and begin to love him just because of who he is? Would he not be overcome by God's free grace that invites us to love him unselfishly?

Loving God just because he is God must become spontaneous and pure in his children. Such love is expressed not only verbally but also in deed. By loving our neighbor and by how we use this world's goods we return God's love. When we love in this way, then we love as God has loved us. No longer do we love God for what we might selfishly gain, but we seek the things that are of Christ and that are to his benefit, just as he sought not his own well-being but our own.

BERNARD OF CLAIRVAUX, *ON LOVING GOD*, CHAP. 9

O MY LORD AND MOST MERCIFUL GOD, my Creator, my Salvation, my Life, my Hope, my Consolation, and my Refuge, govern and uphold my power of free choice by your grace and all-merciful loving-kindness, that I may not by an ill use of freedom offend you. Amen.

ANSELM, ARCHBISHOP OF CANTERBURY, *BOOK OF MEDITATIONS AND PRAYERS*, MEDITATION 19, SEC. 98

FOR REFLECTION: Pss. 34:8; 49:18; 118:1; Matt. 25:35-40; Luke 10:47; John 3:18; 4:42; 15:12; Gal. 6:2; James 1:17; 1 Pet. 1:22; 1 John 3:18; 4:19-20

117

To love our neighbor's welfare as much as our own is true charity out of a pure heart, a good conscience, and a transparent faith. Whosoever loves another in order to seek his own prosperity is exposed as not loving the good for its own sake. One person praises God because God is powerful, another because his gifts are bountiful, and yet another simply because of God's essential goodness. The first person is a slave to fear. The second is greedy and lusts for more benefits. But the third person is a true child of God who honors his Father. The first two types are driven by self-interest.

Neither fear nor self-interest can transform one in God's image. Fear and self-interest may change a person's appearance to make him look like a child of God, and may even modify his conduct, but will never change his heart. A slave may do God's work, but because he toils involuntarily, he remains a slave. A mercenary may serve God, but because he places the price of gain on his service, he remains chained to greed. Where there is self-interest, there is isolation. Fear constrains the slave, and greed the selfish person. But the love that characterizes the child of God never keeps a record of anything of its own.

BERNARD OF CLAIRVAUX, *ON LOVING GOD*, CHAP. 12

O LORD AND SAVIOR, from whom we have all received one blessing after another, here and everywhere, now and always, arrange the days of our lives in the order of your good pleasure, and by your Holy Spirit direct our hearts, tongues, and actions by your mercy in accordance with your will. May we truly study by your grace to speak and to do what pleases you. Amen.

ANSELM, ARCHBISHOP OF CANTERBURY, *BOOK OF MEDITATIONS AND PRAYERS*, MEDITATION 18, SEC. 91

FOR REFLECTION: Pss. 19:7; 49:16-19; 118:1; Matt. 6:24; 13:44; Luke 12:15; John 12:4-6; 1 Cor. 13:5; Phil. 4:11-12; Col. 3:5; 1 Tim. 1:5; 1 John 4:8

118

One law is associated with the spirit of servitude. Its disposition is fear. There is another law having to do with the spirit of liberty. Its disposition is tenderness and love. The children of God do not live according to the first law. And they cannot live without the second. Paul explained that we have received a "spirit of adoption," not the "spirit of bondage" and "fear," by which we name God as our Father. So it is incorrect to say that the righteous have no law, but simply that the law of servitude does not apply to them. The law of fear is imposed on rebels. The law of love is given to God's obedient children. The God who is love is its Author. That is why Jesus could say, "Take my yoke upon you." He meant, "I will not impose my yoke upon you if you are reluctant, but if you will, you may bear it." Under any conditions other than loving obedience, the yoke of Christ produces weariness instead of rest for our souls.

BERNARD OF CLAIRVAUX, *ON LOVING GOD*, CHAP. 14

O GOD, FOUNT AND ORIGIN, Giver and Preserver of all virtues, increase in me, I beseech you, true faith, unfailing hope, and perfect charity; profound humility, invincible patience, and perpetual chastity of body and mind. Give me wisdom, justice, fortitude, and temperance; discretion in all things, and a watchful sensibility, that I may wisely distinguish between good and evil. Amen.

ANSELM, ARCHBISHOP OF CANTERBURY, *BOOK OF MEDITATIONS AND PRAYERS*,
MEDITATION 18, SEC. 90

FOR REFLECTION: Matt. 11:29-30; **Rom. 8:15**; 1 Cor. 9:20; Gal. 4:1-9; Phil. 2:12-15; 1 Tim. 1:9

119

We are told "perfect love casts out fear." But in fact love is never without a fear that is godly. Godly fear doesn't destroy loving devotion. Rather, when mixed with such devotion, godly fear refines devotion. Then the oppressive burden of fear that was once unbearable, because it was slavish, becomes bearable. Godly fear is pure and filial. By contrast, servile fear generates suffering—the cause and its effect. Moreover, love is never without desire, but now it is desire governed by love.

Love perfects the law of service by infusing devotion, just as it perfects the law of wages by restraining covetousness.

Self-interest is restrained within proper boundaries when governed by love. It will now reject evil things and prefer the good. It will be satisfied with the good only as it promotes the better. Similarly, by God's grace God's people will care for their bodies, not as ends in themselves, but in service to the human spirit. And they will cultivate the well-being of the spirit only as it promotes worship of God.

Bernard of Clairvaux, On Loving God, chap. 14

Almighty, eternal, just, and merciful God, grant us the grace to do for you alone all that we know you want us to do and always to desire what pleases you. Thus inwardly cleansed and enlightened, and inflamed by the fire of the Holy Spirit, may we be able to follow in the footprints of your beloved Son, our Lord Jesus Christ. And by your grace alone, may we make our way to you, Most High, who lives and rules in perfect Trinity and simple Unity and is glorified, God all-powerful forever and ever. Amen.

Francis of Assisi, "Letter to All the Friars" (ca. AD 1224),
The Writings of St. Francis of Assisi

FOR REFLECTION: Pss. 34:9-11; 89:7; 111:10; Prov. 8:13; 19:23; Isa. 8:12-13; Matt. 5:17; 10:28; Luke 12:4-5; 2 Cor. 5:11-15; 7:1; **1 John 4:18**

HILDEGARD OF BINGEN

In the medieval church, women could gain a voice as visionaries and prophets if their visions and prophecies were properly validated by ecclesiastical authority. Hildegard of Bingen (AD 1098–1179) was the most important twelfth-century female visionary and prophet. Because of what God permitted her to see, hear, and understand; her literary and administrative gifts; and her leadership as an abbess, Hildegard exercised astonishing influence in the church.

Hildegard was the tenth child of a noble and well-connected family. When she was eight years old, her parents presented her to the church as a tithe. She was placed in the care of noble women whose hermetical dwelling was attached to a male Benedictine monastery. Although Hildegard seems to have been mostly self-taught, she gained a thorough knowledge of the Latin Bible and was able to explore and faithfully articulate orthodox Christian doctrine. Her literary production is astonishing. She wrote almost four hundred letters to almost everyone of importance, as well as to ordinary folk. She wrote texts dealing with theology, botany, and medicine. She also produced a liturgical drama, songs, and poetry. As if this were not enough, she founded two monasteries. In 2012, Pope Benedict XVI named Hildegard a doctor of the church, one of only four women to receive the title.

In *Life*, a work she dictated while in her midseventies, Hildegard says that from childhood she received pictorial visions accompanied by flashes of light and excruciating pain. The visions happened even as she retained consciousness. Afterward, the visions and their meanings were stamped on her memory.

At age forty-two, God instructed Hildegard to record her visions. She did this in *Scivias* (fr. Latin, *Scito vias Domini* [Know the ways of the Lord]). *Scivias* contains twenty-six visions organized into three books. A "declaration that these are true visions flowing from God" opens the *Scivias*. The work contains vivid illustrations of the visions, which are subsequently explained. Hildegard gives a poetic account of each vision. Then she repeats and explains each sentence or phrase.

Hildegard's *final visionary work was the Book of Divine Works,* inspired by an overpowering vision of divine love.

120

And why is [the Son of God] . . . called the Word? Because, just as a word of command uttered by an instructor among local and transitory human dust is understood by people who know and foresee the reason he gave it, so also the power of the Father is known among the creatures of the world, who perceive and understand in Him the source of their creation, through the Word Who is independent of place and imperishable in His inextinguishable eternal life; and as the power and honor of a human being are known by his official words, so the holiness and goodness of the Father shines through the Supreme Word.

HILDEGARD OF BINGEN, SCIVIAS, BK. 2, VISION 1, SEC. 5

O HOLY BREAD! Living Bread! Pure Bread! Only begotten of the Father by the Spirit! Fill us with the fruits of righteousness to the glory and praise of the Father. Even as the angels daily feed on you, may we who are pilgrims to that fair land also feed on you fully; may we daily be refreshed by your nourishment so that we faint not by the way. Though the outward person perishes, feeding on the living Bread, you will renew us day by day. Amen.

FROM A PRAYER BY AMBROSE, BISHOP OF MILAN, FOR SATURDAY, IN "PRAYER BEFORE MASS," WILLING SHEPHERDS OF JESUS CHRIST

FOR REFLECTION: John 1:1-18; 6:35-66; 7:25-53; 8:12-59; 17:1-26; Col. 1:15-20; Heb. 1:1-14

121

(Hildegard offers a vision of the exalted Christ and his church.)

And He makes His way into the greatest height of inestimable glory, where he radiates in the plenitude of wonderful fruitfulness and fragrance. This is to say that the Son of God ascended to the Father, Who with the Son and the Holy Spirit is the height of lofty and excelling joy and gladness unspeakable; where that same Son gloriously appears to His faithful in the abundance of sanctity and blessedness, so that they believe with pure and simple hearts that He is true God and Man. And then indeed the new Bride of the Lamb was set up with many ornaments, for she had to be ornamented with every kind of virtue for the mighty struggle of all the faithful people, who are to fight against the crafty serpent.

HILDEGARD OF BINGEN, *SCIVIAS*, BK. 2, VISION I, SEC. 17

O INEXHAUSTIBLE FOUNTAIN OF ALL GOOD, grant me to recognize your providence that works for our good in all things and to recognize that your many gifts are but your hands taking hold of us in all grace. Enable me by your Spirit, out of love, to offer to you all that I am—all that I have or own, my family, my church, and myself—to do with as you will in accordance with your eternal counsels, the purposes of your grace, and the designs of your glory in all creation. Amen.

FOR REFLECTION: Mark 16:9-20; Luke 24:45-53; Acts 1:1-11; Eph. 1:15-23; 1 Tim. 3:16; Rev. 4:1-11; 5:6-14; 19:6-8; 22:7-21

FRANCIS OF ASSISI

Christians admire no post-New Testament saint more than Francis of Assisi (AD 1182–1226). But his early life predicted that he would be remembered as the privileged, spoiled, and careless son of wealthy parents, not as one who lived a life of poverty in service to the poor and who founded the Franciscan order.

Francis was born the son of a wealthy cloth merchant in Assisi. Later his father changed Francis's baptismal name, Giovanni, to Francesco. The boy received minimal and ineffectual instruction from priests in Assisi. By all counts, as a young man Francis was indulgent and uninterested in pursuing his father's trade. Handsome and charming, he hosted lavish parties. His friends labeled him "king of feasts." Interest in things eternal seemed nonexistent. His keener interests were chivalry and military fame. At age twenty he fought in a war between Assisi and Perugia and was wounded and taken prisoner. His father rescued him, but not before Francis had spent one year in prison, where he contracted malaria.

This experience aroused in Francis the first stirring of things eternal. But upon recovery, his religious sensitivity faded and his thirst for chivalrous fame returned. He set out to join Count Walter of Brienne in battle. But at Spoleto, Francis learned of his hero's death. Despondent, his malaria returned. One evening a mysterious voice told Francis that he was serving the wrong "master." Francis knew that God had spoken and would not turn him loose. Over the next two years, God prepared Francis for conversion. One day, while riding his horse, Francis overtook a leper. Rather than toss the leper a coin and ride away, Francis dismounted, embraced the leper, and gave him all his money. This was Francis's crowning moment of conversion. On his deathbed, in language reminiscent of Paul and Augustine, Francis testified that what had seemed bitter had become sweetness. Grace had won.

Following the encounter with the leper, while Francis was praying in an abandoned church, God told him, "Go and repair my ruined house." Slowly, Francis realized that God had instructed him to rebuild Christ's body. To that calling Francis resolutely submitted.

122

(The following two selections are part of the twenty-eight Admonitions *of Saint Francis, likely delivered to his brother Franciscans.)*

Admonition 2: The Evil of Self-will. The Lord God said to Adam: "Of every tree of paradise you shall eat. But of the tree of knowledge of good and evil you shall not eat." Adam is permitted to eat from every other tree in paradise. As long as he did not disobey the Lord's command, he would not sin. One who eats from the tree of the knowledge of good and evil elevates his own will above God's will and prides himself over goods God created and works in him. Yielding to the devil's temptation, he transgresses the Lord's commandment and experiences evil and guilt. It is thus necessary that he bear the punishment.

Admonition 6: Of the Imitation of the Lord. Brothers, let us consider the Good Shepherd, who to save his sheep bore the suffering of the cross. The sheep of the Lord followed him in tribulation and persecution and shame, in hunger and thirst, in infirmity and temptations, and in all other ways. For following him in this way they received everlasting life from the Lord. Therefore, it is a great shame for us, the servants of God, that while the saints actually did such things, we wish to receive glory and honor by merely telling of their deeds.

FRANCIS OF ASSISI, "THE ADMONITIONS OF ST. FRANCIS," FRANCISCAN MISSIONARIES OF THE ETERNAL WORD

Name him, brothers, name him, with love strong as death,
But with awe and wonder, and with bated breath!
He is God the Savior, he is Christ the Lord,
Ever to be worshipped, trusted, and adored. Amen.

CAROLINE M. NOEL (1817-77), HYMNARY

FOR REFLECTION: Gen. 2:15–3:20; Ps. 138:6; Prov. 6:16-23; Matt. 20:21-28; 24:46; John 10:1-18; 1 Cor. 3:18; Heb. 13:20-21; 1 Pet. 2:20-25; 5:4

123

Admonition 7: Good Works Should Accompany Knowledge. The apostle says, "The letter kills, but the Spirit quickens." They are killed by the letter who learn the Scriptures so that they can be judged as more learned than others and that they may thereby gain riches for their relatives and friends. They are killed by the letter who will not obey the spirit of the Scriptures but instead want to know only the words in order to impose them on others. But they are quickened by the spirit of Scripture who do not interpret it selfishly. By word and deed they return everything to God from whom every good proceeds.

Admonition 13: On Patience. The servant of God cannot know how much patience and humility he has so long as everything is going well. But when those who should do him justice do just the opposite, he has only as much patience and humility as he demonstrates in that moment.

Admonition 15: Peace. "Blessed are the peacemakers: for they shall be called the children of God." They are truly peacemakers who amid sufferings still maintain peace in soul and body for the love of our Lord Jesus Christ.

Francis of Assisi, "The Admonitions of St. Francis,"
Franciscan Missionaries of the Eternal Word

O God Almighty, Lover of humankind, mercifully hear our prayers and supplications. So accept our petitions to assist us and give us the desires of our hearts that are for our advantage. Reveal the gospel of your Christ. Give us illumination and understanding; instruct us in the knowledge of God; teach us your commandments and your ways; implant in us your pure and saving fear. Amen.

Clementine Liturgy (late fourth century),
in Constitutions of the Holy Apostles, bk. 8, sec. 2.6

FOR REFLECTION: Matt. 5:9; 6:2-8; 22:2-33; 1 Cor. 1:26-31; **2 Cor. 3:1-6**; 6:4-6; Gal. 5:1-26; 6:12-16; Phil. 2:3-11; Col. 3:12-13; Heb. 6:1-20

124

Admonition 24: On True Humility. Blessed is he who shall be found as humble among his subjects as if he were among his masters. Blessed is the servant who always continues under the rod of correction. He is a "faithful and wise servant" who does not delay to punish himself for all his offenses, inwardly by a contrite spirit and outwardly by confession and by works of love.

Admonition 25: Of True Love. Blessed is he who loves his brother as much when he is ill and not able to assist as he does when the brother is well. Blessed is he who would love and respect his brother as much when he is away as when he is near.

Admonition 27: How Virtue Drives Out Vice. Where there is charity and wisdom, there is neither fear nor ignorance. Where there is patience and humility, there is neither anger nor disturbance. Where there is poverty with joy, there is neither covetousness nor avarice. Where there is inner peace and meditation, there is neither anxiousness nor dissipation. Where there is fear of the Lord to guard the house, there the enemy cannot gain entry. Where there is mercy and discernment, there is neither excess nor hardness of heart.

FRANCIS OF ASSISI, "THE ADMONITIONS OF ST. FRANCIS,"
FRANCISCAN MISSIONARIES OF THE ETERNAL WORD

O GRACIOUS AND MERCIFUL FATHER, by the indwelling Spirit, open the ears of our hearts that we may exercise ourselves in your law day and night; strengthen us in piety; unite us to, and number us with, your holy flock. Make us to be partakers of your divine mysteries, through Christ, who is our hope, who died for us, by whom glory and worship be given to you in the Holy Spirit forever. Amen.

CLEMENTINE LITURGY (LATE FOURTH CENTURY),
IN *CONSTITUTIONS OF THE HOLY APOSTLES*, BK. 8, SEC. 2.6

FOR REFLECTION: Isa. 12:2; **Matt.** 5:3-10; 6:25-34; **24:45**; Luke 11:21; Rom. 14:17-19; 1 Cor. 13:1-13; Phil. 4:2-9; Col. 3:15

125

("The Canticle of the Sun")

Be praised, my Lord, by all your creatures,
Especially through Brother Sun,
Who brings the day; you give light through him.
He is beautiful and radiant in all his splendor!
Of you, Most High, he bears a likeness.
Praise be to you, my Lord, through Sister Moon
And the stars in heaven, for you made them,
Clear and precious and beautiful.
Praise be to you, my Lord, through Brother Wind,
And through the air, cloudy and serene,
And every kind of weather through which
You give sustenance to all your creatures.
Praise be to you, my Lord, through Sister Water,
Which is very useful and humble and precious and chaste.
Praise be to you, my Lord, through Brother Fire,
Through whom you light the night; he is beautiful
And playful and robust and strong.
Praise be to you, my Lord, through Sister Mother Earth,
Who sustains us and governs us and who produces
Varied fruits with colored flowers and herbs.
Praise be to you, my Lord,
Through those who give pardon because of your love.

. . . .

Praise and bless my Lord,
And give him thanks,
And serve him with great humility. Amen.

FRANCIS OF ASSISI, "CANTICLE OF BROTHER SUN," PRAYER FOUNDATION

FOR REFLECTION: Exod. 15:2; Judg. 5:3; Pss. 7:17; 33:4-9; 65:8-13; 69:34; 89:5; 98:4; 104:1-35; 148:1-14; Rom. 8:22-25; Rev. 5:12

MEISTER ECKHART

One of the most controversial medieval theologians had a profoundly positive impact on Christian spirituality. Meister Eckhart (ca. AD 1260–ca. 1327) lived an influential and stormy life as writer, teacher, and administrator. His appeal continues, as is evidenced by a flourishing Meister Eckhart Society and lively publications about him. Dag Hammarskjöld, former secretary-general of the United Nations, kept Eckhart's works at bedside.

Johannes Eckhart was the greatest medieval German mystic. At around age fifteen he joined the Dominican order and studied theology. He was strongly influenced by the great Dominican Thomas Aquinas (ca. 1225-74) and also by Neoplatonism, a source that led to challenges to Eckhart's orthodoxy.

Eckhart's abilities were harnessed for numerous assignments. After a period spent teaching, from 1294 to 1298, he served as prior (head of a religious order) of the convent of Erfurt. Concurrently, he filled the office of vicar of Thuringia. In 1302, his order awarded him the master of sacred theology degree. In 1303, Eckhart was elected provincial of the province of Saxony and was reelected in 1307. He was also appointed vicar-general of Bohemia. In 1311, Eckhart resumed his teaching at the University of Paris. From 1314 to 1317, he taught and preached in Strasbourg and preached in Cologne. In 1317, Eckhart became prior at Frankfurt and, in 1320, returned as professor of his order at Cologne.

Eckhart's writings examine the relationship between the individual soul and God. His way of explaining the relationship sometimes got him into trouble; some of his teachings seemed pantheistic (i.e., there is no essential difference between God, the world, and the soul, there being only a single divine essence that comprises everything). Mysticism of this sort tries to transcend the "apparent difference" between God and the soul. In 1326, Eckhart recanted some of his propositions. He died at Avignon in 1327 while attempting to defend his orthodoxy before the pope. He had walked five hundred miles to do so. Modern scholars consider Eckhart's mysticism generally orthodox. In August 1992, the master of the Dominican order, Fr. Timothy Radcliffe, pronounced Eckhart "a good and orthodox theologian."

126

The works of the Holy Trinity in creation and redemption are inseparably joined. When the Father draws us, he draws us to his Son. When the Son draws us, he draws us to the Holy Spirit. The Holy Spirit draws us to the Father and the Son. When each person draws us to the two other persons, he also draws us to himself because there is one Godhead. We are drawn by the triune God with cords of power, wisdom, and love. The Father draws us by the goodness of his grace and thereby demonstrates his measureless power. The Son draws us and thereby shows his unfathomable wisdom, for he is the Wisdom of the Father. The Holy Spirit draws us by his steadfast love.

The Son descended from heaven to become incarnate in the Virgin Mary. He fully took on himself our humanity, our bodily weaknesses, yet without sin. From his words, works, passion, limbs, and nerves, Christ fashioned a mighty cord. Then with bloody sweat dripping from his sacred brow, he used the cord to draw us to himself. He laid aside all his glory, was stretched upon a cruel cross, and there defeated everything that wants to obstruct his drawing us to redemption.

MEISTER ECKHART, "THE ATTRACTIVE POWER OF GOD,"
IN *MEISTER ECKHART'S SERMONS*, SERMON 1

GLORY BE TO THE FATHER,
Who by his almighty power and love created us.
Glory be to the Son,
Who by his precious blood rescued us from the dominion of darkness.
Glory be to the Holy Spirit,
Who faithfully bears witness to Christ
And daily sanctifies the church of God as promised. Amen.

FOR REFLECTION: Hos. 2:16-23; 11:1-4; 14:4-9; John 3:16-18; 6:41-51; Rom. 11:33; 16:25-27; 1 Cor. 1:18-31

127

The kingdom of God is *near* us; it is also *in* us. What does it mean for the kingdom of God to be *in* us? If I were a king, but had no knowledge of being a king, would I really be a king? But if I were fully convinced of being a king, and everyone affirmed my kingship, then I would surely be a king. All the wealth of kingship would be mine.

Similarly, our salvation depends on our *knowing* and *affirming* the Chief Good, which is God himself.

Our joy arises, not from the *fact* that God is *near*, but from truly *knowing* him, from *knowing* his presence, and because he possesses us. Our joy increases or diminishes according to our *knowledge* that God loves us.

The kingdom is none other than the coming of God himself, bringing all his riches. When we come to *know* God's kingdom is not only *near* us but *in* us, we will need no human agency to convince us; we will be assured within by the gift of eternal life. Then we will be able to say with Jacob, "God is in this place, and I did not know it."

Meister Eckhart, "The Nearness of the Kingdom,"
in *Meister Eckhart's Sermons*, sermon 2

O Master, Christ our God, King of the ages, and Maker of all things: We thank you for the privilege of participating in the life-giving mystery of salvation. By the power of the Holy Spirit keep your church under your protection, in the shadow of your wings. Grant to us with a pure conscience to be strengthened with power and patience and joyfully to give thanks to the Father, who has made us inheritors of the kingdom of light. Blessed is the kingdom of the Father and of the Son and of the Holy Spirit. Amen.

FOR REFLECTION: Gen. 28:10-17; Matt. 5:3, 10; 6:9-13; Mark 9:45-47; Luke 8:1; 17:20-21; 18:17; 21:29-36; Col. 1:9-23; 1 Thess. 2:12

128

Grace is God's gift; it operates in the depth of the soul that employs this gift. Grace is a light that goes forth; it serves under guidance of the Holy Spirit. The Spirit's divine light permeates the soul and raises it above the turmoil of temporal things, to rest in God. We receive the light of God by which the soul advances as though we had received a nuptial gift from Christ. Natural light causes flowers and plants to grow. The light of the Holy Spirit shining in Jesus' disciples yields the fruit of blessedness.

Fire converts wood into its own likeness, even so God's love forms his likeness in us. The peace, freedom, and blessedness God promises come from abiding in his will. Toward this perfect union the soul strives perpetually. We know the stronger the wind blows, the larger a fire becomes. Now understand that love is the fire in our souls and that the Holy Spirit fans the flame. The freer the Holy Spirit is to work in us, the brighter becomes the fire of love. The soul grows gradually in Christ's likeness by God's grace.

MEISTER ECKHART, "OUTWARD AND INWARD MORALITY,"
IN *MEISTER ECKHART'S SERMONS*, SERMON 7

MAKE SHINE IN OUR HEARTS, O Master who loves humankind, the incorruptible light of your divine knowledge, and open the eyes of our mind to comprehend the proclamation of your gospel. Instill in us also the fear of your blessed commandments, that, trampling down all carnal desires, we may pursue a holy way of life, both considering and doing all things well-pleasing to you. To the Father, the Son, and the Holy Spirit we send up glory, now and ever, and unto ages of ages. Amen.

JOHN CHRYSOSTOM, IN *THE DIVINE LITURGY OF ST. JOHN CHRYSOSTOMOS*,
THE ORTHODOX CHRISTIAN PAGE

FOR REFLECTION: John 1:16-17; 8:10-14; 12:44-50; Rom. 3:23-24; 5:14-21; 1 Cor. 15:9-11; 2 Cor. 3:3; 4:6; 8:7-9; Gal. 4:6; 1 John 4:4-10

129

To produce real moral freedom, God's grace and man's will must cooperate. Just as God is the Prime Mover of nature, even so he creates in us the power to move freely toward himself. Grace sets our wills free so we may do everything, working by grace. So the will arrives at true freedom through love, or more correctly, it *becomes* love, for love unites the will with God. All true Christian morality, inward and outward, has love as its substance; love is the foundation of all God's commandments.

Morality must be built on this foundation, not on self-interest. As long as morality is built on something other than love for God, it is not free, for then it lacks that inner freedom that manifests itself in works of love. True freedom is the government of nature inside and outside through God. Love often begins with fear. But it must not end there. Fear is like the awl that draws the shoemaker's thread through the leather; the end is love.

No external law is needed for the righteous person, because he fulfills the law inwardly. He bears the law in his spirit. This is intended for those who are enlightened by God and the Holy Scriptures.

Meister Eckhart, "Outward and Inward Morality,"
in *Meister Eckhart's Sermons*, sermon 7

O Spirit of Life, O Spirit of God,
Enlighten us by that same Word;
Teach us to know the God's radiant love;
Lead us to Christ who reigns above:
O Spirit of Life, O Spirit of God. Amen.

Johann Niedling (1602-68), trans. John Caspar Mattes (1913), Hymnary

FOR REFLECTION: Matt. 22:34-40; Luke 12:48; John 8:32; Rom. 8:1-17; 12:1-2; 13:8-10; 1 Cor. 15:10; Gal. 2:19-21; 5:1-6; Phil. 3:7-11

130

Outward as well as inward morality helps form true Christian freedom. We are correct to lay primary emphasis on the inner person. But in this world there is no inner holiness without its outward expression. The inner work is first of all the work of God's grace in the depths of the human spirit. But that grace and that work must be distributed throughout the whole person, in our reason as faith made strong, in our will as love for God and neighbor, and in our desire as steadfast hope. When the divine light penetrates the human spirit, the human spirit is united with God as light unites with light. This is the light of faith, wrought by God's grace, that elevates us to heights of free obedience unobtainable by human efforts alone.

Our spirits should be turned toward God even as we turn to face the sun to absorb its warmth. Then we can absorb God's love. As God can only be seen by his own light, so he can only be loved by his own love. Through the Holy Spirit all the redemptive graces are implanted in our human features. The Spirit transfers us out of sin and into the life of grace.

The essence of morality *resides in the inner*, not the outer, *person*, the *intensity of the will* from which it springs, and the *nobility of the aim* for which it is practiced.

MEISTER ECKHART, "OUTWARD AND INWARD MORALITY,"
IN *MEISTER ECKHART'S SERMONS*, SERMON 7

> OH! FOR A CLOSER WALK WITH GOD,
> A calm and heavenly frame;
> A light to shine upon the road
> That leads me to the Lamb! Amen.
>
> WILLIAM COWPER (1731–1800), HYMNARY

FOR REFLECTION: Rom. 5:1-10; 8:18-28; 15:13-14; Eph. 1:15-23; 2 Cor. 5:16-21; 2 Thess. 1:1-12; 1 Pet. 4:1-11; Jude vv. 12-25

JOHN OF RUYSBROECK

Monica the mother of Augustine, Anthusia the mother of John Chrysostom, and Susanna the mother of John Wesley represent mothers who played major roles in shaping Christian leaders. The mother of John of Ruysbroeck (ca. AD 1293–1381) is another. From John's infancy she trained him in the way of Christian holiness. Born at Ruysbroeck near Brussels, he was the greatest of the Flemish (a group of Dutch dialects spoken in the historic region of Flanders) mystics. His writings are considered classics of Christian spirituality.

At age eleven John left home and became a student of his saintly uncle, John Hinckaert, a priest and canon of St. Gudule's, Brussels. Along with a fellow priest, Francis van Coudenberg, Hinckaert had committed to living in apostolic simplicity. The education John of Ruysbroeck received prepared him for the priesthood. He was ordained in 1317. For twenty-six years John, the uncle, and van Coudenberg lived in austerity and monastic retirement. John continued his studies and wrote books that would become the foundation for his teaching. His masterpiece was *The Spiritual Espousals*, consisting of three books that treat the active, the interior, and the contemplative life.

During this time, John defended orthodox faith against doctrinal errors being propagated by the Brethren of the Free Spirit. Partly because of opposition resulting from his defense of the faith, and partly out of a desire for more solitude, John, along with his uncle and van Coudenberg, moved to a hermitage near Soignes, Belgium. Numerous disciples followed, resulting in the formation of a monastery. John was made the prior (head of a religious order). Works written by him during this period were *The Sparkling Stone*, *The Little Book of Enlightenment*, and *The Book of the Twelve Beguines*.

John's form of mysticism generated troubling questions about his orthodoxy. Some passages sound pantheistic (i.e., the belief that there is no essential difference between God and his creation). Others seem to deny that God is essentially and eternally triune. But on balance, the church has judged him orthodox. During his lifetime, his writings were eagerly received and his renown as a spiritual teacher spread throughout Holland, Germany, and France.

131

Some people receive the gifts of God as hirelings; others, as his faithful children. They differ in intention, feeling, and love, and in every movement of the interior life.

Those who love themselves so inordinately that they will not serve God unless there is promise of reward actually separate themselves from God. They are slaves to their own selfishness, for in seeking God they, in fact, promote themselves. In their prayers and good works they lust after physical rewards. Or perhaps they strive for eternal things, but for selfish reasons.

Turned inward, such persons dwell alone. They lack the true love that could unite them to God and to their neighbor. They abide by the law and commandments but are strangers to the law of love. Their obedience proceeds, not from love, but from a desire not to be damned. Because they are inwardly unfaithful, such people dare not trust God. Prayers and good works, practiced to get rid of fear, are of no help at all, for the more they love themselves, the more they fear hell. Their fear springs from self-love, not from love for God.

There is a solution for such a miserable way of life. The one thing lacking is a pure love for God himself that overturns self-sovereignty. Such love requires an inwardly transformed life.

JOHN OF RUYSBROECK, *THE SPARKLING STONE*, CHAP. 6

O LORD MY GOD, give ear to my prayer, and let your mercy hearken to my desire, because it is anxious not for myself alone but would serve brotherly charity. I would sacrifice to you the service of my thought and tongue; give me what I may in turn offer you. For "I am poor and needy"; you are rich to all that call on you. You are not troubled by care, but you care for us. Amen.

AUGUSTINE, BISHOP OF HIPPO, *CONFESSIONS*, BK. 11, CHAP. 2, SEC. 3

FOR REFLECTION: Deut. 11:13-15; **Pss.** 37:4; **86:1**; Matt. 19:16-22; Luke 6:27-38; John 14:15-21; Rom. 15:1-3; 1 Cor. 2:9; 2 Cor. 5:14-15; 1 John 3:17

132

Compassion is an inward movement of the heart, stirred by pity for the spiritual and physical needs of others. The manifold sorrows of our Lord move Christians to compassion. The manifold oppressions of the poor; the grief caused by loss of family, friends, goods, honor, and peace; and the countless sorrows that fall upon humankind will move the righteous to compassion.

He who is compassionate is a sign of Christ's sufferings, his choosing the cross, his love, his wounds and tenderness, the grief and shame he endured. Christian compassion bears witness to the nails in our Lord's hands, to his crown of thorns, and to his mercy shown to the crucified thief.

Compassion should lead a Christian to look into himself. True compassion moves us to confront our failures, the opportunities we have wasted, and our moral imperfections. Such honesty makes compassion authentic. Compassion also marks the errors and disorders of our fellow human beings and moves us to pray for their salvation.

God ordained compassion before all the virtues. This is why Christ said, "Blessed are they that mourn, for they shall be comforted."

JOHN OF RUYSBROECK, *THE ADORNMENT OF THE SPIRITUAL MARRIAGE*, BK. 1, CHAP. 18

O LORD JESUS, you have told us in your Word that we can understand God's love by how you laid down your life for us. And you have told us plainly that on the great day of judgment you will not recognize anyone as being one of your own, who does not recognize your presence in those who hunger and thirst, in strangers and the naked, in the sick and imprisoned. Mold us so that on that great day you will recognize the love of God dwelling in us. Amen.

FOR REFLECTION: Matt. 5:4; 9:36-38; 18:23-34; 25:31-46; Luke 10:25-37; Gal. 6:2; Eph. 4:19; Col. 3:12; James 2:1-13; 1 Pet. 4:10; 1 John 3:14-18

133

From compassion springs generosity. Generosity is a liberal flowing forth of a heart touched by charity and pity. It springs from reflecting on the compassion, sufferings, and sorrows of Christ. Such reflection prompts us to praise and worship our Lord for his love and for his pains. In joyful and humble surrender we give ourselves to him—body and soul, for time and eternity.

If a Christian reflects on the good God has done for him, and considers his own failures, then he must pour himself into the generosity of God. Becoming a generous person follows from taking refuge in God's faithfulness and mercy and from turning to him in a trust bent on serving the Lord forevermore. Such a Christian prays to God with ardent faith. Divine gifts will generously flow to others through him. The hope is that as a result people will turn to the truth and come to know our Redeemer.

The generous person will mark with compassion the needs of others. With prudent discretion, he serves, gives, lends, and consoles insofar as he is able.

JOHN OF RUYSBROECK, *THE ADORNMENT OF THE SPIRITUAL MARRIAGE*, BK. I, CHAP. 19

I PRAY WITH ALL MY HEART AND VOICE TO YOU, O God the Father of our Lord Jesus Christ, that your bounteous grace will enable us to perceive in the incarnation of your Son both your gift and his love and that all may understand the truth that for us, your Son, our Lord God, was born and suffered and rose again. May his condescension ever produce in us an increase of love. Grant us to rightly and wisely comprehend the blessings of our Redeemer's compassion. Amen.

JOHN CASSIAN, *SEVEN BOOKS ON THE INCARNATION OF OUR LORD*, BK. 7, CHAP. 31

FOR REFLECTION: Matt. 5:42; 6:1-4; 25:34-40; Luke 3:10-11; 6:38; Acts 20:35; 2 Cor. 8:7-9; Eph. 4:28; 1 Tim. 6:17-19

JULIAN OF NORWICH

Like Melchizedek, whose importance outstrips our information about his life, we know little about the English mystic Julian of Norwich (ca. AD 1342–ca. 1416). She was probably a Benedictine nun who lived most her life as an anchorite (a person who takes a vow to retire to seclusion for a life of prayer and contemplation) in a small room attached to St. Julian's Church in Norwich, then a large and prosperous city. Julian devoted her life to prayer and meditation. Were it not for her book *The Sixteen Revelations of Divine Love*, she would probably be unknown.

On a single day in 1373 Julian received fifteen visions and another one the following day. In 1393, she wrote the book that records and explains her ecstatic visions of divine love. Caught up in rapture that characterizes the mystical experience, Julian was shown visions of our Lord's passionate sufferings and of the Trinity. For twenty years she carefully reflected on their meaning: they disclosed the depths of God's unconditioned love for us, manifest in Jesus Christ. Julian was able to perceive how understanding God's love offers answers to life's question, particularly the presence of evil in the creation.

The visions themselves are somewhat baffling. Only by hearing Julian explain them can we understand what she saw. She was probably influenced by *The Cloud of Unknowing*, a fourteenth-century book about Christian mysticism. She was also influenced by a philosophy know as Neoplatonism, a philosophy that eventually became a synthesis of Platonism and Christian theology and that in some forms had a keen interest in the soul rising to union with God.

In the closing paragraph of her *Revelations of Divine Love*, Julian summarizes her visions: "I saw with certainty that even before God created humankind, he loved us, that his love has never lessened, nor will it ever. All God's works, including the creation, are performed in love. He has made all things profitable for us. Although we had a beginning, God's love is everlasting. All of this we shall see without end" (chap. 86).

134

The Lord gave me a vision of his tender love. I saw that in all ways he is good and beneficent. His love is the clothing that wraps us, holds us, and encloses us.

The Lord placed in my hand a small round ball the size of a hazelnut. I asked, "What does this mean?" He answered, "It represents the whole creation." As I looked, I feared that the little piece might disappear. The Lord answered, "It will not disappear; it is made secure by my love. The whole creation is enclosed in my love."

I learned three things about the creation. God made it, he loves it, and he keeps it. I can never be completely at rest or fully experience the Lord's joy until this becomes true of me: God is my Maker, my Lover, and my Keeper. There must be no distance between God's love and me.

Failing to rest in God, who is almighty, all-wise, and all-loving, we seek rest in finite things. The Lord is our Rest, and it pleases him when we fully trust him. In nothing less can peace be found. We cannot have rest until we are emptied of things that falsely claim to give peace.

JULIAN OF NORWICH, *REVELATIONS OF DIVINE LOVE*, REVELATION 1, CHAP. 5

O GOD, ALL YOUR WORKS PRAISE YOU. Permit me to be numbered among your holy ones, to resemble them in virtue and aspiration and to sit with them at the feet of Jesus. May my faith be grounded in your Word, my understanding enlightened by your Spirit, all my aspirations be holy, my motives examined by you, and my heart always harmonized with your will. May my life display your resources and adorn the doctrine of God. Amen.

FOR REFLECTION: Pss. 24:1-2; 31:19; 33:5; 34:1-22; Nahum 1:7; John 1:1-5; Rom. 8:28; 11:36; 1 Cor. 8:6; Col. 1:15-20; Heb. 11:4; Rev. 4:11

135

God showed me that it is far more important to worship him, to delight in his goodness, and to cling to his grace than to worry about the mechanics of prayer. True prayer involves learning to cling to God's goodness in steadfast love. It is possible to concentrate so much on "how" to pray that we are robbed of worship and of resting in God's goodness.

We thank him for the love he showed on the cross, his unending kindness, and the eternal life he bestows. We praise him for the church triumphant, for saints who have preceded us to glory and who pray for us before the Father. He delights when we seek him and worship him.

Exulting in God's goodness is the highest form of prayer. His goodness reaches the depths of our needs, he gives us his life, he strengthens us in his grace, and he cultivates Christian virtue in us. God despises nothing he created. Truly his love surpasses comprehension.

God wills that we be occupied with knowing him and exploring his love until our knowledge and love are made perfect in heaven.

JULIAN OF NORWICH, *REVELATIONS OF DIVINE LOVE*, REVELATION 1, CHAP. 6

As Isaac carried firewood for the burnt offering, likewise Christ carried the wood of the cross. As Isaac returned alive, likewise you O Christ rose living, from the dead, and appeared to your holy disciples. May you now bless us so that with a pure heart, an enlightened soul, an unashamed face, a faith unfeigned, a perfect love, and a firm hope, we may dare with boldness, without fear, to pray to you, O God, our Holy Father. Amen.

BASIL THE GREAT, "HOLY THURSDAY," *ST. BASIL LITURGY*, COPTICCHURCH.NET

✠✠✠

FOR REFLECTION: 1 Chron. 16:32; Ps. 64:8; Isa. 49:13-23; Matt. 6:5-15; Luke 11:9-13; Eph. 6:8; Phil. 4:4, 6-7; James 5:16; 1 John 5:14-15

136

(Julian has been permitted to understand the holy awe that seized the Virgin Mary at the annunciation.)

When Mary beheld the glory of the Lord, she was filled with holy fear. She was struck by her unworthiness. How could she, so lowly and so simple, become the mother of our Lord? At the same time, she was filled with the grace and truth of God.

How incomprehensible that God, who is so holy, so mighty, and so terrifying, is yet so loving, so gracious, so comforting, and so attentive.

The Lord explained this to me. What if a mighty king were to reveal himself to one of his poor servants? What if the king were to act graciously toward him, take him into his private counsel, and with good cheer fully reveal himself to his servant? How would the servant respond? He would say, "What more could my mighty lord have done for me? What could inspire more worship and joy than that my lord has revealed himself to one so lowly, so simple? This brings more joy than if he had bestowed expensive gifts."

And should not our hearts be even more ravished by joy over the great kindness our Lord Jesus Christ has shown? Our greatest joy should be that he, though the highest and mightiest, the most noble and worthy, in the incarnation became for us the most humble, the most gracious, and the most redemptive.

JULIAN OF NORWICH, *REVELATIONS OF DIVINE LOVE*, REVELATION 1, CHAP. 7

O MY GOD, Father of our Lord and Savior Jesus Christ, enlighten me with your saving faith, gladden and strengthen me with your joyful and never-faltering hope, and quicken me with your mighty and all-holy love. Amen.

FOR REFLECTION: Pss. 75:1; 106:1; 136:1-3; Isa. 53:1-12; Matt. 9:2-7; Luke 1:46-55; 8:22-25; 14:15-24; Rom. 5:1-10

137

I heard these words: "The enemy is overcome." Then I was permitted to see in Christ's passion on the cross how he suffered all the scorn and malice that sin and Satan could hurl his way. But our Lord returned an even greater contempt and opposition against Satan, so much so that he defeated that ancient foe.

Today, Satan harbors the same malice against Christ and his people as before the incarnation, especially as he sees our Lord spoiling Satan's kingdom and setting his captives free. Christ turns Satan's attacks on Christians into joy and blessings. He shames the tempter. Satan's power to harm Christians has itself been taken captive by our Lord. Just as Christ has successfully scorned Satan's malice and wickedness, he wills that by divine power his disciples will do the same.

Having seen our Lord's contempt for Satan's malice, having seen him decisively break Satan's power, and after hearing this is the power and pattern by which Christians should live, we should break out in raucous laughter over the magnitude of Christ's victory and Satan's defeat. Christians should laugh at Satan. Such victorious laughter by God's children gives me great pleasure.

JULIAN OF NORWICH, *Revelations of Divine Love*, REVELATION 5, CHAP. 13

Dear Savior of the world, assist us to rejoice in you, the Strength of our salvation, the Cause of our freedom, the Price of our redemption. We were captives, but you have redeemed us; we were slaves, but you set us free; we were exiles, but you brought us home; we were dead, but you restored us to life. Hallelujah! In this and the life to come, our joy shall be full. Amen.

ANSELM, ARCHBISHOP OF CANTERBURY, *Book of Meditations and Prayers*, MEDITATION 11, SEC. 52

FOR REFLECTION: Matt. 28:16-20; Luke 8:26-39; 9:37-43; 10:17; Rom. 8:37-39; 16:17-20; Col. 2:13-15; James 4:7; Rev. 19:1–20:10

138

Insofar as Christ is the reigning Head of the church and its members, he is glorified and his work is complete. But insofar as he desires the redemption of all persons, Christ's work is incomplete. He continues to have the same desire, thirst, and longing he had while suffering on the cross. He will continue to have this thirst until the last person who will be redeemed has been redeemed.

Just as God demonstrates compassion and pity, even so in him there is a thirst and longing for the redemption of all persons. Apart from God's longing, no person could come to the Redeemer. God's compassion and pity, thirst and longing, spring from his boundless goodness; it draws us up to his bliss.

JULIAN OF NORWICH, *Revelations of Divine Love*, REVELATION 13, CHAP. 31

O Holy God, who rests in the saints; who is praised with the thrice-holy hymn by the seraphim and is glorified by the cherubim and worshipped by all the heavenly hosts; who brought all things into existence from nothing; who has created humankind according to your own image and likeness and adorned him with your every gift; who gives wisdom and understanding to all who ask and who does not reject sinners but provided repentance that leads to salvation; who has enabled us, your lowly and unworthy servants, to offer the worship and glory due to you. O Master, forgive our transgression, sanctify our souls and bodies, and grant us to serve you in holiness all the days of our lives. Amen.

JOHN CHRYSOSTOM, *The Divine Liturgy of St. John Chrysostom*, ORTHODOX.NET

FOR REFLECTION: Mark 13:1-37; John 3:16; Rom. 8:18-25, 37-39; 1 Cor. 15:20-28; 2 Thess. 2:1-17; 2 Pet. 2:9; Rev. 22:12-17

139

When a person sets his will to love God with all his heart, he may be assured that God loves him more. It is God's love that causes divine grace to work abundantly in us. He wills that his people be as assured of the eternal joys in heaven while we live here below as we will be on the day we see our Lord face-to-face. In fact, the more joy and pleasure we receive from such anticipation and assurance, the more it pleases our heavenly Father. With holy reverence and godly humility we live in the guarantee of that hope.

The Lord is now graciously present with us; we see him as marvelously great and ourselves as marvelously small. Accordingly, the virtues of holy fear and humility mark those who walk righteously before the Lord. As we walk, God's presence cultivates in us the assurance of true faith, charity, and a *fear* of the Lord that is, ironically, *full of joy.*

God desires that we see ourselves as bound to him by his love, which can create such a unity between Christians and their Lord that they could not conceive of departing from him. This is the marvelous work of the Lord in those who fully love him.

JULIAN OF NORWICH, *REVELATIONS OF DIVINE LOVE*, REVELATION 15, CHAP. 65

It is meet and right to hymn you, to bless you, to praise you, to give thanks to you, to worship you in every place of your dominion, for you are God inexpressible, incomprehensible, invisible, unattainable, ever existing, eternally the same, your only begotten Son and your Holy Spirit. You raised us up again and did not cease to do all things until you had brought us up to heaven and had bestowed on us your kingdom, which is to come. For all these things we give thanks to you, to your only begotten Son, and to your Holy Spirit. Amen.

JOHN CHRYSOSTOM, *THE DIVINE LITURGY OF ST. JOHN CHRYSOSTOM*, ORTHODOX.NET

FOR REFLECTION: Matt. 5:20; Luke 1:67-80; John 6:53-57; 10:27-29; Rom. 5:7-21; 8:37-39; Eph. 3:7-21; Heb. 3:6, 14; 12:28-29; 1 John 4:7-12; 5:14

CATHERINE OF SIENA (CATERINA DI BENINCASA)

What can a woman who lives only thirty-three years contribute to Christ's body? Catherine of Siena (AD 1347-80) answers. In her short life and thereafter, she exercised immense influence. Not only did she leave a legacy of letters and celestial visions, but her counsel was also sought by Pope Gregory XI and his successor Urban VI. She negotiated with politicians, princes, and ecclesiastical powers to resolve a seventy-year-old schism in the church. Her influence and legacy are so great that in 1970 Pope Paul VI conferred on her the title doctor of the universal church, one of only four women so honored. A doctor of the church is someone whose writings are judged so orthodox that they can be used in church teaching.

Born in Siena, Italy, to a father whose trade was dying cloth and a mother who was a poet, Catherine was the youngest of twenty-four surviving children. Throughout her life she suffered periods of intense pain, perhaps caused by migraine headaches. From childhood, Catherine received visions of Christ, which she recorded and explained. Her first vision occurred when she was six. The result was that she gave her life to devotion and took the vow of chastity at age seven. At age fifteen, Catherine took the habit of the Dominican tertiary sisters and began the religious practice of a hermit in a room in her home. After three years, during a visit to the city of Pisa, Catherine received the stigmata of Christ (marks similar to the wounds of the crucified Christ in her flesh) from a wooden cross hanging in a church. In 1370, she received a series of visions of divine mysteries and heard God tell her to leave her hermit's cell to serve as his emissary in the world. Catherine tirelessly ministered to the poor and those suffering dread diseases, wrote instructive letters to persons of all social ranks, wrote and traveled to mediate disputes in the papacy, and recorded her visions. Around 1377, Catherine founded the monastery of Santa Maria degli Angeli in the castle of Belcaro. Her contemporaries bore witness to her charm, maintained even during times of pain and persecution. She is entombed in the Church of Santa Maria sopra Minerva (Rome).

140

Make two homes for yourself, my daughter: one home in your cell and the other a spiritual home you must always carry. This is the house of self-examination. There you will seek knowledge of God's goodness.

Actually, these two houses are one; when abiding in one, you should also be abiding in the other. Otherwise, you would be overcome by either confusion in the one house or arrogance in the other. If you trust in your own assessment of yourself, then confusion about who you really are will follow. On the other hand, if in religious isolation and exaltation you stay in the other house and ignore what you truly know about your whole self, you will fall into spiritual pride.

You see that the two houses must be built together and integrated. If you do this, you will be perfected in love. By dwelling in the one, you will gain knowledge of your human weaknesses as well as your strengths. By dwelling in the other, you transparently bring your failures before the loving Lord. You will not receive judgment and rejection from him.

From such holistic honesty about oneself before the Lord there flows a stream of humility that will safely bring both sorrow and consolation. A person who integrates both parts of his life will be conformed to the crucified Christ.

CATHERINE OF SIENA, "TO MONNA ALESSA DEI SARACINI,"
IN *THE LETTERS OF CATHERINE BENINCASA*

LORD, take me from myself; give me to yourself. I commend my heart to your watchful care, for I know its vulnerability. Cause me to be a mirror of your grace, to show others the joy of your salvation. Teach me the discipline of attending to things temporal with a mind intent on things eternal. Amen.

FOR REFLECTION: Pss. 51:1-19; 139:1-24; Luke 9:62; 14:28-31; 2 Cor. 13:5; Gal. 6:3-5; James 1:23-25; 1 Pet. 1:13

141

Those who are fully committed to Christ have uprooted perverted pride and the leaven of impatience. Carnal pride is the beginning of every sin. Christ's disciples must expel their rebellious self-wills that spring from carnal pride. They must give free reign to divine grace. Instead of being ruled by pride, self-will, and impatience, Jesus' disciples must bear in their hearts the crucified Christ, must rejoice in his wounds, and must desire nothing above him.

There is no true Christian obedience without humility, and no humility without love. All this was modeled by our Lord. In humility before his Father, Christ willingly bore the shameful cross. Nails would not have been enough to hold the God-man; only love could have kept him there. Because Christ's disciples know all this, they should seek no joy apart from the crucified Christ. Even if they could gain eternal life, escape hell, attain holiness, and receive spiritual and material consolation without being crucified with Christ, they would reject it.

Because Jesus' disciples know that only love and obedience held him to the cross, in reciprocal love they should be ready to be clothed with his shame, for they have been invited to the table of the spotless Lamb and will settle for nothing less.

Oh, glorious fellowship! Who would not give himself to death a thousand times to gain it?

Catherine of Siena, "To Monna Agnese, Who Was the Wife of Messer Orso Malavoti," in The Letters of Catherine Benincasa

O Lord God Almighty, we beseech and entreat you to perfect within us your grace. Pour out through our hands the gift of your pity and compassion. Amen.

Adaeus and Maris, The Liturgy of the Blessed Apostles (ca. AD 150)

FOR REFLECTION: Matt. 26:36-46; Luke 14:11; Acts 2:36; Rom. 12:3; 1 Cor. 1:23-25; 2 Cor. 11:30; Eph. 2:10-22; Phil. 2:3-11; Heb. 12:1-3

142

The lost sheep had been held captive by Satan. Then the infinite goodness of God came along, beheld the sheep's ruinous situation, and saw the sheep could not be rescued by venting divine wrath, for the sheep deserved an incomprehensible penalty. Rather, the highest and eternal wisdom of God looked for an attractive and gentle way to rescue the sheep and saw that the human heart is highly attracted by love, because in love, God created humanity. The Father, therefore, seeing humanity so ready to love, threw the book of love straight at the lost sheep by giving the Word, his only begotten Son.

You see, divine justice had earlier come along and demanded punishment be exacted for sins committed. But divine mercy and unspeakable charity showed up. To satisfy justice and the gravity of sin, mercy led the Son to the cross, having first fully clothed him in the clay of sinful Adam. On the cross, the incarnate Word pacified divine wrath and rescued the lost sheep from Satan's bondage. Using the wood of the cross, Christ jousted with death, sacrificed himself, and destroyed our death. Oh, the divine love that returned the sheep to the fold!

CATHERINE OF SIENA, "TO GREGORY XI," IN
THE LETTERS OF CATHERINE BENINCASA, SECOND LETTER TO GREGORY

O GOD, nail down our flesh with a godly fear, and let not our hearts be inclined to words or thoughts of evil, but pierce our souls with your love, that ever contemplating you, being enlightened by you, and discerning you, we may unceasingly render worship and gratitude to you, the eternal Father, with your only begotten Son, and your all-holy and life-giving Spirit. Amen.

FROM A PRAYER OF BASIL THE GREAT, IN THE ORTHODOX PRAYERS

FOR REFLECTION: Luke 24:1-7; John 3:10-18; 10:11-18; Acts 2:36-39; Rom. 5:6-8; 8:35-39; 1 Cor. 2:9; 2 Cor. 13:14; Gal. 2:20; Phil. 2:8; Col. 1:15-20; Heb. 13:20-21; 1 John 3:1-3

THOMAS À KEMPIS

Thomas à Kempis (ca. AD 1380–1471) figures prominently among those in church history who have influenced the meaning of Christian discipleship. Next to the Scriptures, his *Imitation of Christ* has been translated into more languages than any other book. Its influence has endured over five hundred years. Were ecclesiastical or secular position required for making a deep impact on the formation of Christian character, Thomas à Kempis would be excluded. Most of his long life was given to the practice of monasticism. His influence sprang from a life devoted to prayer and the examination of what is required of and promised to Jesus' followers.

He was born in the Rhineland town of Kempen, near Düsseldorf in Germany. He attended school at nearby Deventer, in the Netherlands, where he was known as Thomas of Kempen. The school was founded by Gerard Groote, who also established the Brothers of the Common Life. The Brothers of the Common Life gave themselves to prayer, a simple life, and union with God. Thomas was captivated by the quality of piety his teachers exhibited, so much so that he determined to make their ideals the pattern for his life. At age nineteen he entered the monastery of Mount St. Agnes near Zwolle, the Netherlands. There he would spend the rest of his life. As a monk, he conducted Mass, heard the confessions of visitors to Mount St. Agnes, and spent most of his time reflecting on what being formed in Christ's image means. From time to time he was given administrative responsibilities, but only temporarily. From his gifted capacity for intense reflection flowed sermons, hymns, letters, and descriptions of the lives of the saints. *The Imitation of Christ* is his most important work. John Wesley (1703-91) was among the Christian stalwarts influenced by the book. In 1735, he translated and published the book as *The Christian's Pattern*. Although Wesley turned away from the mysticism

Thomas à Kempis represented, nevertheless in 1738 he credited the book with teaching him that "true religion was seated in the heart, and that God's law extends to all our thoughts as well as words and actions" (*"The Imitation of Christ" through Six Centuries*).

143

What good does it do to speak as one highly learned about the Trinity if, lacking humility, we displease the Trinity? It is a virtuous life that makes us holy, just, and pleasing to God. I would rather experience contrition than merely be able to define and discuss it. What profit would there be in knowing the Bible by heart, and the principles of all the philosophers, if we were to live as paupers to God's grace and love? Everything is vanity unless one loves and serves God.

The greatest wisdom is to seek the kingdom of heaven through contempt for anything that would lead us away. It is vanity to court honor and to be puffed up with pride. It is vanity to follow the lusts of the body and desire things for which severe punishment will follow. It is vanity to wish for long physical life but then care little about living a well-invested life. It is vanity to be anxious about the present and not to make provisions for the world to come. It is vanity to love what passes quickly and not look ahead to eternal joy.

THOMAS À KEMPIS, *THE IMITATION OF CHRIST*, BK. 1, CHAP. 1

GRANT ME YOUR GRACE, O most merciful Christ, so that I may always seek to make your will my own. Let me be unable to will or not will anything but what you will or do not will. Above all desires, give me the desire to rest in you. In you alone let my heart have peace. Without you all things are difficult and troubled. In the peace that is in you, the Most High, the everlasting Good, I will sleep and take my rest. Amen.

THOMAS À KEMPIS, *THE IMITATION OF CHRIST*, BK. 3, CHAP. 15

FOR REFLECTION: Matt. 6:19-34; 13:44-45; 16:24-27; Mark 7:20-23; 9:47; John 8:12; Gal. 5:16-26; Col. 1:9-14; James 4:1-5; 1 John 3:18-22

144

Shun idle talk as much as possible, for discussion of worldly affairs, even though important, can be a great distraction. We are too easily ensnared and too quickly preoccupied by such things.

Many are the times when I have wished I had held my peace and had not associated with certain people. Why, indeed, do we converse and gossip among ourselves when we so often conclude with a troubled conscience? We do this because we seek affirmation from each other. We talk endlessly and speak fondly of things that please us or of things we intensely dislike. But sad to say, we often talk vainly and with no purpose at all. Such pointless chatter effectively subverts inward divine consolation.

When the right and opportune moment comes for speaking, say something that will be truly beneficial.

Bad habits and indifference to spiritual progress do much to remove the guard from the tongue. On the other hand, devout conversation about spiritual matters promotes growth in the Lord when carried on between brothers and sisters in Christ who deeply love the Lord.

THOMAS À KEMPIS, *THE IMITATION OF CHRIST*, BK. I, CHAP. 10

ALMIGHTY AND EVERLASTING GOD, who in the paschal mystery established the new covenant of reconciliation: Grant that all who are reborn into the fellowship of Christ's body may show forth in their lives what they profess by their faith; through Jesus Christ our Lord. Amen.

"THE LITURGY OF THE WORD," THE GREAT VIGIL OF EASTER, IN BCP

FOR REFLECTION: Pss. 19:14; 141:3; Prov. 15:28; Eph. 4:15, 29; 5:4; Col. 2:6-19; 3:27; 2 Tim. 2:14-16; James 3:2-10; 6; Rev. 3:7-13

145

As long as we live in this world, we will not escape suffering and temptation. We learn from Job that "the life of humans on earth is a warfare." Everyone must diligently guard against temptation and watch in prayer lest the devil, who goes about seeking whom he may devour, find occasion to deceive us. No one is so holy that he is never tempted.

Temptations, though troublesome and severe, are often useful. Through them we can be humbled, purified, and instructed.

Many people try to flee from all temptations, only to fall more deeply into them. We do not conquer by fleeing. Through patience and humility we become stronger than our enemies. The person who fails to deal with temptations at their roots only appears to confront them. He will make little spiritual progress. Indeed, temptations will return more quickly and violently.

Little by little, in patience and long-suffering, we overcome temptations. We do this with God's help instead of by punishing ourselves or acting impulsively. Be prepared to receive counsel, and don't be harsh with others who are tempted, but console them as you would want to be consoled.

THOMAS À KEMPIS, *THE IMITATION OF CHRIST,* BK. I, CHAP. 13

O CHRIST JESUS, who freely took on yourself the form of a servant and became obedient to death on the cross, teach us that if we are to come directly, safely, and openly to you without hindrance, freely and peacefully, and be securely joined to you with a fervent spirit, whether in prosperity or adversity, in life or in death, then we must commit everything unhesitatingly and resolutely to your benevolent and infallible will. Amen.

ATTRIBUTED TO ALBERT THE GREAT, *ON CLEAVING TO GOD,* CHAP. 16

FOR REFLECTION: Job 7:1-10; Matt. 9:6-13; 26:41; Luke 8:13; Rom. 12:2; 1 Cor. 10:13; Gal. 5:16; Heb. 4:14–5:3; 1 Pet. 5:8; 1 John 1:9; 2:1; 4:1

146

Just as a rudderless ship is driven aimlessly by the waves, so a careless and irresolute person is tempted and tossed in many directions. But for a disciplined Christian, just as fire tempers iron, so temptation can temper the righteous. Often we do not know what we can endure, but temptation reveals our substance.

Above all, we must be especially alert against temptations as they begin. Satan is more easily conquered if he is quickly refused admission into the mind. He should be confronted at the door as soon as he knocks.

Someone has said correctly, "Resist the beginnings; remedies come too late. By long delay, evil gains strength." First, a mere thought comes to the mind. Then imagination blossoms and is followed by evil delight and then consent. Thus, if Satan is not confronted at the threshold, he will gain full entry. The longer the delay, the weaker the response, and the stronger the enemy becomes.

Let us not despair, therefore, when we are tempted but pray to God the more fervently that he may see fit to help us, for according to the apostle Paul, the Lord will assist us to resist temptation.

THOMAS À KEMPIS, *THE IMITATION OF CHRIST*, BK. I, CHAP. 13

O MY GOD, Light of the blind and Strength of the weak, Light of those that see and Strength of the strong, we turn to you, for we know you are present when we converse with you and when we cast ourselves on you. You, who created us, recreate us and grant that we may love you perfectly, even to the end of the ages. Amen.

AUGUSTINE, BISHOP OF HIPPO, *CONFESSIONS*, BK. 11, CHAP. 2, SEC. 3

FOR REFLECTION: Prov. 4:23; Isa. 55:2; John 9:4; Rom. 12:2; 1 Cor. 10:11-13; 15:58; Gal. 6:7-10; Heb. 6:10-12; 2 Pet. 1:3; 2:1-3; 3:15

147

Carefully examine yourself and be slow to judge the deeds of others. Our judgment is often a mistaken and wasted effort. Judging ourselves is usually more profitable. Often we judge others on the basis of how we think things ought to be. We usually do this based on our own limited and subjective notions. Consequently, objective perspective is easily lost.

If our love for God were our primary interest, we would not be so easily disturbed by opposition to our opinions. We too easily permit peripheral interests to drag us along with them. Many people identify themselves by their external activities. They appear to enjoy peace of mind so long as their external world is in order. But when that world goes awry, they easily become disoriented and dispirited.

Admittedly, old habits are hard to break. But if we find ourselves relying on our own intelligence and industry and on shifting external interests, instead of on discipline by the Lord Jesus, we should not be surprised if we fail to be guided by Christ's wisdom. God wants us to rise above what human wisdom produces and through ardent love be completely subject to and enlightened by him.

THOMAS À KEMPIS, *THE IMITATION OF CHRIST*, BK. 1, CHAP. 14

MY LORD AND SAVIOR, you said if we love you and keep your commandments, we will be kept by you, through the Holy Spirit, to the glory of the Father. May I be kept to do your will, kept to do your work in your own way, kept, it may be, to suffer for your sake, kept that you may do with me what seems good to you, and kept so that no other lord shall ever have dominion over me. Amen.

FRANCIS HAVERGAL, *KEPT FOR THE MASTER'S USE*, CHAP. 1

FOR REFLECTION: Ps. 118:1-29; Prov. 3:5-6; Isa. 12:2; Matt. 6:25-34; Phil. 1:6-7; 4:6-7; Heb. 13:6; 1 Pet. 5:6-7; Rev. 7:1-17

148

There is no shortage of those who want the Lord's consolation, but there are too few of those who will endure the trials of discipleship. Everyone wants Jesus to make them happy; too few are willing to suffer anything for his sake. Many applaud our Lord's miracles; too few are willing to bear the reproach of the cross. Many people praise and bless the Lord as long as he heaps delights upon them.

Those who serve the Lord in order to receive benefits and consolation are religious mercenaries, hirelings, always concentrating on the pay they will receive. Their constant anticipation of profit and gain shows they love themselves more than they love the Lord.

But those who love Jesus for his own sake and not for selfish gain and comfort will bless the Lord in times of trial and anguish. Oh, what power there is in a pure love for Jesus.

THOMAS À KEMPIS, *THE IMITATION OF CHRIST*, BK. 2, CHAP. 11

O MY GOD! I offer you all my actions of this day for the intentions and for the glory of the sacred heart of Jesus. I desire to sanctify every beat of my heart, my every thought, my simplest works, by uniting them to Christ's infinite merits; and I wish to cast them into the furnace of his merciful love.

O my God! I ask of you for myself and for those whom I hold dear, the grace to fulfill perfectly your holy will, to accept for love of you the joys and sorrows of this passing life, so that we may one day be united together in heaven for all eternity. Amen.

THÉRÈSE OF LISIEUX, "A MORNING PRAYER," IN *STORY OF A SOUL*

FOR REFLECTION: Ps. 24:16; Matt. 11:29; 14:25-35; Luke 9:23-27; 17:10; 1 Cor. 6:19-20; Phil. 2:5-8; 2 Tim. 2:8-13; 1 Pet. 2:21-25

149

(The Royal Road of the Cross)

For many Christians, Jesus' instruction "Deny yourself, take up your cross, and follow me" seems unbearable. But it will be much more unbearable to hear Jesus say, "Depart from me, you cursed, into everlasting fire." Those who now hear the word of the cross and who willingly obey it have no reason to fear the day of judgment. When the Lord comes to judge, the sign of the cross will be in the heavens to comfort them. All servants of the cross who have made themselves one with the crucified Lord will joyfully draw near to Christ the Judge.

Why, then, would we be reluctant to walk the royal road of the cross when by it we can journey to the kingdom of heaven? In that cross there is salvation; in the cross is life; in the cross is protection from the enemies of our souls; in the cross is infusion of heavenly communion; in the cross is strength of mind; in the cross is joy; in the cross is the highest virtue; and in the cross is holiness perfected.

Only along the royal road of the cross is there to be found salvation. Sisters and brothers, let us take up the cross and follow Jesus. By following him we shall enter eternal life.

THOMAS À KEMPIS, *THE IMITATION OF CHRIST*, BK. 2, CHAP. 12

ALMIGHTY GOD, whose most dear Son went not up to joy but first he suffered pain, and entered not into glory before he was crucified: Mercifully grant that we, walking in the way of the cross, may find it none other than the way of life and peace; through Jesus Christ our Lord. Amen.

"THE LITURGY OF THE PALMS," THE SUNDAY OF THE PASSION: PALM SUNDAY, IN BCP

FOR REFLECTION: Isa. 50:4-7; **Matt. 16:24**; **25:41**; Luke 9:23-27; 14:27; 19:28-36; 22:14-23; 23:1-49; Phil. 2:6-11

150

Jesus opened the road of the cross. His entire life moved along this road. Would we then seek a road of ease? It is true that the way of the cross is not what we would naturally choose. If we were to rely on ourselves, we would have nothing to do with it. Only as we trust in the Lord will courage be given. Only then will the natural man be made subject to the Spirit. Only the grace of God, not human virtue, can cause us to love what we naturally reject.

Let us bravely bear the cross of our Lord, who out of love was crucified for us. With reciprocal love let us drink the cup of the Lord. Leave consolation to God; let him do with us as is most pleasing.

Even if with Paul we were to be elevated to the third heaven, we would not be excused from the way of the cross. Paradoxically, the royal road is a "dying life," for the more a Christian dies to himself, the more he lives in Christ. No one is fit to enjoy heaven who has not resigned himself to that road. If there had been some other way, the Lord would have shown it.

Thomas à Kempis, *The Imitation of Christ*, bk. 2, chap. 12

Almighty and Ever-living God, in your tender love for the human race you sent your Son our Savior Jesus Christ to take upon him our nature and to suffer death upon the cross, giving us the example of his great humility: Mercifully grant that we may walk in the way of his suffering and also share in his resurrection; through Jesus Christ our Lord. Amen.

"The Liturgy of the Palms," The Sunday of the Passion: Palm Sunday, in BCP

FOR REFLECTION: Pss. 34:19; 22:24; Luke 9:23-27, 51-56; John 16:33; 17:1-5; Acts 9:1-18; Rom. 5:3-5; 8:18; 2 Cor. 4:8-10; 10:13; 2 Thess. 1:1-13; 1 Pet. 4:12-19; 5:10

THEOLOGIA GERMANICA

In 1516, a year before Martin Luther (1483–1546) posted his Ninety-Five Theses on the door of All Saints' Church in Wittenberg, he discovered and published a work written by an unknown author. The title of the work is *Theologia Germanica*, or *German Theology*. Luther declared, "Next to the Bible and St. Augustine, no book has ever come into my hands from which I have learned more of God and Christ and man and all things that are" (preface to the second edition [1518]). The book was enthusiastically received by Luther's compatriots.

The *Theologia Germanica* comes from a Roman Catholic context and is instructive for all Christians. Even a brief exploration of the book reveals why Luther treasured it so highly. In very practical and doctrinally responsible language, the *Theologia Germanica* examines the work of God's grace and calls Christians to a life of holiness in all aspects of life. Its subtitle is instructive; it "sets forth many fair aspects of divine Truth and voices many excellent and lovely things about Christian perfection." The work's confidence in the transforming and enabling grace of God is, as Luther discovered, at many points simply breathtaking.

Although the work is anonymous, it likely arose from within a group of Christians known as the Friends of God (see John 15:15). Members of the association were male and female, clergy and lay. They were characterized by a vital piety that included a life of self-denial and the recognition of the worthlessness of religion that did not deeply transform its practitioners, for no one can truly know God who does not love him fervently and who does not partake of the divine nature. The *Theologia Germanica* reveals that the Friends of God believed strongly in the Holy Spirit's presence and work in all Christians. The work is organized into fifty-four chapters.

151

Not even God himself can make a person virtuous, good, or happy, so long as virtue and goodness are only exterior qualities, alien to one's character. Failure to internalize these qualities happens when one becomes so absorbed in the affairs of this world, and is so captivated by its values, that he can't withdraw to examine himself. He lacks the ability to nurture his own soul by engaging in transforming fellowship with the Lord.

Therefore, although it is good to learn what the saints have suffered and accomplished, and how God provided for them, it would be a thousand times better to learn who we are before the Lord and what he requires of us. The premier question is, "How may our lives be placed in the Lord's service so that he can use us just as he did the saints?" To know ourselves transparently before the Lord is the highest art. That will make us more commendable before the Lord than if we could understand all there is to know about humans, the heavens, and the earth.

Eternal blessedness is to be found in holy obedience before the Lord.

THEOLOGIA GERMANICA, CHAP. 9

OUR FATHER IN HEAVEN, instill in us through your Holy Spirit a love for you, motivated not by command but by a new nature that instructs and prompts us to render unavoidable worship and praise. May our life express your divine life as the natural outgrowth of a newborn soul. May we give thanks, and repent not only because these things are commanded but rather because we are deeply aware of our needs, of the folly of sin, and of your divine goodness. Amen.

HENRY SCOUGAL, *THE LIFE OF GOD IN THE SOUL OF MAN*, PT. 1

FOR REFLECTION: Pss. 51:10-11; 139:3-4; Matt. 5:13-26; John 3:1-15; 2 Cor. 3:18; 5:17; Gal. 2:20; 5:19-26; 1 John 3:2-6

152

Let no one think he can attain new life in Christ by debating the terms of discipleship or by secondhand knowledge. Neither will a person attain true life in Christ by just reading about him, by achieving great learning, or by practicing exalted religious techniques. One who is bent on advancing his own religious opinions or who serves the Lord for selfish reasons will never come to new life in Christ. Our Lord made all of this clear when he said, "If any man will come after me, let him deny himself and take up his cross and follow me." He was telling us plainly that unless a person is prepared to forsake all prior conditions, claims, and requirements he has made on God, he will not attain eternal life. As long as a person clings to bits and pieces derived from a fallen world instead of surrendering himself to Jesus Christ, he will continue to be deceived and blinded. The problem is that such a person requires discipleship be tailored for his own convenience. Instead of following Jesus on his terms, such a person elevates what he judges to be worthwhile above Christ himself.

THEOLOGIA GERMANICA, CHAP. 19

O LORD JESUS, by the Spirit of our heavenly Father, cause your peace to rule in our hearts and your word to dwell in us richly. Make our enjoyment of this life to be with a good conscience, our endurance of death to be with the hope of immortality, and our assurance of the resurrection to encourage us through grace. May truth be with us in simplicity, faith with confidence, abstinence with holiness, industry with soberness, conversation with modesty, and learning without vanity. Instill in us fidelity to true doctrine. Amen.

FROM AN ADMONITION BY AMBROSE, BISHOP OF MILAN, *LETTERS*, EPISTLE 63, SEC. 113

FOR REFLECTION: Matt. 16:24; 10:38; Mark 8:34; 10:21; Luke 18:18-25; Rom. 12:1; Gal. 2:20; 5:24; 6:14; Eph. 4:11-17; James 1:19-27

153

Someone might ask, "What does it mean to partake of the divine nature as Peter commended?" Or what does it mean to be a godly person? It means to be *illumined* through and through by the eternal and divine light. It means to be *inflamed* or *consumed* by divine love.

But you must understand that light and knowledge are worthless apart from love. Call to mind that even though a person is skilled at knowing the difference between virtue and evil, if he does not love virtue, he will not be virtuous. If he loves virtue, he will pursue it; he will be enlisted as an enemy of evil. And if he truly loves virtue, he will not leave a single virtue unattended. Furthermore, while living virtuously, he will require no reward and would accept no treasure in exchange; love of virtue is itself sufficient reward. In fact, to gain the whole world a virtuous person would not surrender being virtuous. He would rather die a miserable death than surrender virtue.

THEOLOGIA GERMANICA, CHAP. 41

DEAR SAVIOR, through the gracious work of the Holy Spirit, nurture in us that divine life that becomes an inward, free, and self-motivating principle so that we may be moved to love and obedience, not by external motives, threats, bribes, or promises, nor constrained by law, but that we may be powerfully inclined to that which is good and may, because of love, delight in the performance of your will; to the glory of God the Father, through God the Son, and by God the Holy Spirit. Amen.

ADAPTED FROM HENRY SCOUGAL, THE LIFE OF GOD IN THE SOUL OF MAN, PT. 1

FOR REFLECTION: Ps. 1:1-3; Mic. 6:8; Matt. 6:33; Rom. 5:1-5; 12:1; 2 Cor. 6:14-17; Gal. 2:20; Phil. 4:8; 1 Tim. 6:17-19; 2 Pet. 1:1-9

154

Our Lord Jesus Christ said, "No one comes to the Father but by me." Let us carefully consider the conditions by which we might come to the Father through our Lord. A Christian must set a watch over himself and all that belongs to him, whether possessions of the inner person or possessions that mark his outer life. As far as is possible, he must so direct, govern, and guard his heart that neither his will nor his desire, neither love nor longing, neither opinion nor thought, shall spring up in his heart or abide in his actions except those things that would bless God and be pleasing to him. And whenever he becomes aware of any thought or intention in himself that is contrary to God's nature and will, he must resist it and thoroughly root it out as quickly as possible.

By this rule a Christian must order his life, whether he is working or resting, speaking or being silent, waking or sleeping, walking or standing still. In brief, in all ways, whether involved in his own affairs or working for someone else, Jesus' disciple must guard his heart with all diligence. He must permit nothing to dwell within or about him that would be found unacceptable if Christ were to become incarnate again and walk among us.

Theologia Germanica, CHAP. 52

O IMAGE OF THE INVISIBLE GOD, the Firstborn over all creation, in your Father and by the Spirit you have rescued us from the dominion of darkness and brought us into the kingdom of God. Set our hearts on things above, and fill us with all spiritual wisdom and understanding. For to you belongs all glory, honor, and worship, to the Father, and to the Holy Spirit, now and ever. Amen.

FOR REFLECTION: John 10:1, 3; 12:26; **14:6**; Rom. 12:1-2, 9-13; Gal. 5:16-26; Eph. 2:1-10; 5:1-14; Phil. 4:2-9; Col. 1:9-14; 1 Pet. 1:3-11

SOURCES

The reading, prayers, and hymns used in this book were adapted from the following sources:

Albert the Great. "A Prayer from St. Albert the Great on Conscience." A Blog for Dallas Area Catholics. Accessed November 12, 2013. http://veneremurcernui.wordpress.com/2010/08/23/a-prayer-from-st-albert-the-great-on-conscience/.

Ambrose. "A Prayer before Mass (Thursday)." Catholic Online. Accessed November 13, 2013. http://www.catholic.org/prayers/prayer.php?p=2040.

———. Prayer for Saturday. In "Prayer before Mass." Willing Shepherds of Jesus Christ. Accessed November 13, 2013. http://www.willingshepherds.org/Thanks%20Thomas.htm.

———. "Prayers by St. Ambrose." 2 Hearts Network. http://www.2heartsnetwork.org/Ambrose.htm.

Anselm. *St. Anselm's Book of Meditations and Prayers*. London: Burns and Gates, 1872. Reprint, Christian Classics Ethereal Library. http://www.ccel.org/ccel/anselm/meditations.html.

Augustine. "Prayer for the Indwelling of the Holy Spirit." The Fresh Anointing. http://www.tfadc.org/resources.

———. "Prayer to the Holy Spirit." Feast of All Saints. http://feastofsaints.com/staugustine.htm.

Basil the Great. *St. Basil Liturgy*. CopticChurch.net. http://www.copticchurch.net/topics/liturgy/liturgy_of_st_basil.pdf.

Bennett, Arthur, ed. *The Valley of Vision: A Collection of Puritan Prayers and Devotions*. Carlisle, PA: The Banner of Truth Trust, 1994.

Bonaventure. "Prayers of St. Bonaventure." Liturgies.net. http://www.liturgies.net/saints/bonaventure/prayer.htm.

Book of Common Prayer. New York: Church Hymnal Corporation, 1979. http://justus.anglican.org/resources/bcp/formatted_1979.htm.

A Book of Offices. Milwaukee: Young Churchman, 1914. http://justus.anglican.org/resources/bcp/Offices1914/Offices_1914.htm.

Cassian, John. *The Conferences of John Cassian*. Translated by Edgar C. S. Gibson. Reprint of the 1894 edition, Christian Classics Ethereal Library. http://www.ccel.org/ccel/cassian/conferences.titlepage.html.

Catherine of Siena. The Letters of Catherine Benincasa. Translated by Vida D. Scudder. Reprint of the 1905 edition, Project Gutenberg, 2005. http://www.gutenberg.org/cache/epub/7403/pg7403.html.

Catholic Encyclopedia. Accessed September 16, 2013. http://www.newadvent.org/cathen/.

Chrysostom, John. *The Divine Liturgy of St. John Chrysostom*. Orthodox.net. http://www.orthodox.net/services/sluzebnic-chrysostom.pdf.

———. *The Divine Liturgy of St. John Chrysostomos*. The Orthodox Christian Page. http://www.ocf.org/OrthodoxPage/liturgy/liturgy.html.

———. A prayer. In "Seasonal Prayers: For Lent." Prayers. iBreviary.com. http://www.ibreviary.com/m/preghiere.php?tipo=Preghiera&id=487.

The Divine Liturgies of Our Fathers among the Saints John Chrysostom and Basil the Great. Edited by J. N. W. B. Robertson. London: Nutt, 1894. https://archive.org/stream/divineliturgies00churgoog#page/n5/mode/2up.

Donne, John. *John Donne's Devotions*. 1624. Reprint, Christian Classics Ethereal Library. http://www.ccel.org/ccel/donne/devotions.

Eckhart, Johannes. *Meister Eckhart's Sermons*. Translated by Claud Field. London: H. R. Allenson, [1909?]. Reprint, Christian Classics Ethereal Library. http://www.ccel.org/ccel/eckhart/sermons.

The Eckhart Society. Accessed October 21, 2013. http://www.eckhartsociety.org/eckhart/eckhart-man.

Ephrem the Syrian. "Prayer of Saint Ephrem." *OrthodoxWiki*. Accessed November 13, 2013. http://orthodoxwiki.org/Prayer_of_Saint_Ephrem.

Francis of Assisi. "The Admonitions of St. Francis." Franciscan Missionaries of the Eternal Word. http://www.franciscanmissionaries.com/about-us/admonitions/.

———. "Canticle of Brother Sun." Prayer Foundation. http://www.prayerfoundation.org/canticle_of_brother_sun.htm.

———. *The Writings of St. Francis of Assisi*. Translated by Paschal Robinson, 1905. http://www.sacred-texts.com/chr/wosf/wosf03.htm.

Gregory of Nazianzus. "The Gregory of Nazianzus Prayer." Amos House Community. Accessed November 12, 2013. http://amoshouse.wordpress.com/2011/02/22/the-gregory-of-nazianzus-prayer/.

SOURCES

Gregory the Great. *Morals on the Book of Job*. Oxford: John Henry Parker; London: J. G. F and J. Rivington, 1844. Reprint, Lectionary Central. Accessed October 21, 2013. http://www.lectionarycentral.com/GregoryMoraliaIndex.html.

———. "Prayer of Acclaim to the Suffering Christ." Saints.SQPN.com. Accessed November 13, 2013. http://saints.sqpn.com/pray0540.htm.

Hildegard of Bingen. *Scivias*. Classics of Western Spirituality. Translated by Mother Columba Hart and Jane Bishop. Mahwah, NJ: Paulist Press, 1990.

Hymnary.org. http://www.hymnary.org/texts?qu=+in:texts.

"*The Imitation of Christ* through Six Centuries." Dallas: Southern Methodist University Bridwell Library, 2012. Exhibition catalog. Accessed October 21, 2013. https://www.smu.edu/Bridwell/Collections/SpecialCollectionsandArchives/Exhibitions/ImitatioChristi/1735.

John of Ruysbroeck. *The Adornment of the Spiritual Marriage*. Translated by C. A. Wynschenk Dom. Edited by Evelyn Underhill. 1916. Reprint, Christian Classics Ethereal Library. http://www.ccel.org/ccel/ruysbroeck/adornment.iv.html.

———. *The Sparkling Stone*. Translated by C. A. Wynschenk Dom. Edited by Evelyn Underhill. 1916. Reprint, Christian Classics Ethereal Library. http://www.ccel.org/ccel/ruysbroeck/adornment.v.html.

Julian of Norwich. *Revelations of Divine Love*. Translated by Grace Warrack. 1901. Reprint, Christian Classics Ethereal Library. http://www.ccel.org/ccel/julian/revelations.

Macarius-Symeon. *Fifty Spiritual Homilies of St. Macarius the Egyptian*. Translated by A. J. Mason. London: Society for Promoting Christian Knowledge, 1921. http://archive.org/stream/fiftyspiritualho00pseuuoft/fiftyspiritualho00pseuuoft_djvu.txt.

Newman, John Henry. "A Prayer of John Henry Cardinal Newman." Catholic Newman Center. University of Houston. http://uhcatholic.org/content/article/6024/prayer-john-henry-cardinal-newman.

Nicene and Post-Nicene Fathers, Series I (14 vols.), Series II (14 vols.). Edited by Philip Schaff. Reprint of the 1885 edition. Christian Classics Ethereal Library. http://www.ccel.org/fathers.html.

The Orthodox Prayers. Accessed November 14, 2013. http://ihtys.narod.ru/orthodox_prayers.pdf.

"Prayers to the Holy Spirit." 2 Hearts Network. http://2heartsnetwork.org/HolySpirit.htm.

Saint Vladimir Russian Orthodox Church. *Prayer Book*. http://www.saintprincevladimir.org/spiritual-guides/prayer-book/.

Scougal, Henry. *The Life of God in the Soul of Man*. 1677. Reprint, Christian Classics Ethereal Library. http://www.ccel.org/s/scougal/life/.

St. Thomas Prayers. http://www.stthomas.webhero.com/St-Thomas-Prayer.htm.

Taylor, Jeremy. *The Rule and Exercises of Holy Living.* Philadelphia: J.W. Bradley, 1860. Reprint, Christian Classics Ethereal Library. http://www.ccel.org/ccel/taylor/holy_living.toc.html.

Theologia Germanica. Translated by Susanna Winkworth. Edited by Peiffer. Golden Treasury Series. Reprint of the 1893 edition, Christian Classics Ethereal Library. http://www.ccel.org/ccel/anonymous/theologia.titlepage.html.

Thérèse of Lisieux. *Story of a Soul: The Autobiography of St. Thérèse of Lisieux*. Edited by T. N. Taylor. London: Burns, Oates, and Washbourne, 1912. Reprint, Christian Classics Ethereal Library. http://www.ccel.org/ccel/therese/autobio.

Thomas à Kempis. *The Imitation of Christ*. Translated by Aloysius Croft and Harold Bolton. Milwaukee: Bruce Publishing Company, 1940. Reprint, Christian Classics Ethereal Library. http://www.ccel.org/ccel/kempis/imitation.

Thomas Aquinas. A prayer before Communion. In "Prayers before Holy Communion." Diocese of Superior. http://www.catholicdos.org/file/Prayersbefora&fterHolyCommunion.pdf.

———. "Prayers by St. Thomas Aquinas." 2 Hearts Network. http://www.2heartsnetwork.org/Aquinas.htm.

———. "St. Thomas of Aquinas Quotes." http://misalvador777.tripod.com/catholictreasurechest/id239.html.

Vetter, Herbert F., ed. *Prayers for Today*. Cambridge, MA: Harvard Square Library, 2004. http://www.harvardsquarelibrary.org/Prayers/.

Wesley, John. *A Christian Library*. 1750. Reprint of 1821 edition. 30 vols. Wesley Center Online. http://wesley.nnu.edu/john-wesley/a-christian-library/.

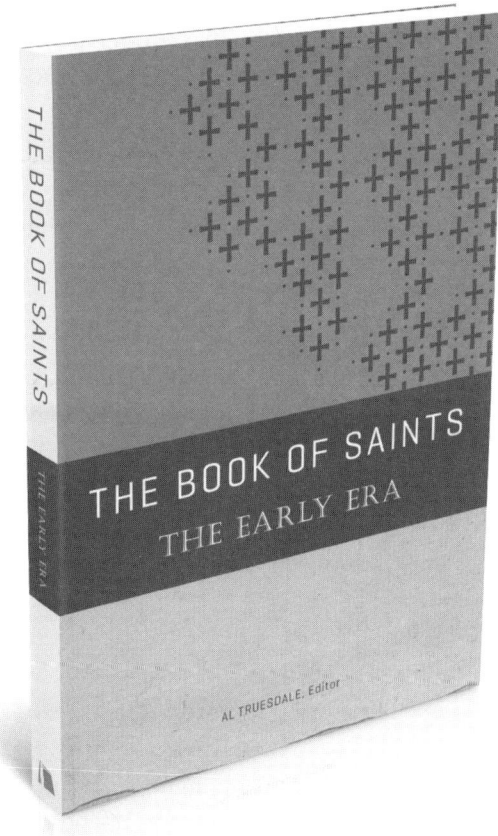

From Christ followers living near the time of the apostles to the early defenders of the faith, we are enriched by the wise advice and inspiring examples of our Christian ancestors. In the face of heresy and persecution, these saints lived lives faithful to the gospel story.

The Book of Saints: The Early Era is a devotional gateway to the thoughts and insights of church leaders and teachers who lived before the middle of the fourth century AD.

The Book of Saints: The Early Era
Al Truesdale
ISBN: 978-0-8341-3006-7

Available online at BeaconHillBooks.com
Also available as an ebook